Faux Florals

easy arrangements for all seasons

Arturo Quintero

Photographs by Andy Ryan

CREATIVE
HOMEOWNER® Home Arts

CRE▲TIVE
HOMEOWNER®

A Division of Federal Marketing Corp.
Upper Saddle River, NJ

FAUX FLORALS

SENIOR EDITOR	Carol Endler Sterbenz
SENIOR GRAPHIC DESIGN COORDINATOR	Glee Barre
"ESSENTIALS" DESIGNER	Amanda Wilson
PHOTO EDITOR	Robyn Poplasky
EDITORIAL ASSISTANTS	Jennifer Calvert and Nora Grace
INDEXER	Schroeder Indexing Services
COVER DESIGN	Glee Barre
PRINCIPAL PHOTOGRAPHY	Andy Ryan
PHOTO ASSISTANT	Mandy Hanigan
INSTRUCTIONAL PHOTOGRAPHY	Steven Mays
PHOTO STYLIST	Sylvia Lachter
PRODUCER OF PHOTOGRAPHY	Genevieve A. Sterbenz
TECHNICAL EDITOR	Emily Harste
TECHNICAL WRITER AND MODEL MAKER	Genevieve A. Sterbenz

CREATIVE HOMEOWNER

VICE PRESIDENT AND PUBLISHER	Timothy O. Bakke
PRODUCTION DIRECTOR	Kimberly H. Vivas
ART DIRECTOR	David Geer
MANAGING EDITOR	Fran J. Donegan

Current Printing (last digit)
10 9 8 7 6 5 4 3 2 1

Faux Florals, First Edition
Library of Congress Control Number: 2006939477
ISBN10: 1-58011-352-4
ISBN-13: 978-1-58011-352-6

CREATIVE HOMEOWNER®
A Division of Federal Marketing Corp.
24 Park Way
Upper Saddle River, NJ 07458
www.creativehomeowner.com

Dedicated to my dear family and many friends

whose encouragement and support have allowed me to be

inspired by the world.

Table of Contents

An Illustrated Glossary of Floral Arrangements

SPRING

Lemonade

First Blush

Spring Joy

SUMMER

Little Black Dress

Meadow in a Box

Sterling Pink

Tropical Paradise

AUTUMN

Rustic Chic

Autumn Sun

Autumn Leaves

Tuscan Sunset

WINTER

Christmas Bazaar

Hot-Pink Holiday

Happy "Holly" Days

Simply Modern

Special Occasion

Spring Parade

Citrus Grove

Fuchsia Fiesta

Sweet Charlotte

Beach House

Sunny Side

French Harvest

Morning Brew

Kitchen Kitsch

Welcome Wreath

White Christmas Wreath

Southern Hospitality

Silver Snowfall

Winter Herb Garden

Introduction

*D*esign is an inherently personal process, with each designer creating myriad reflections of his or her own passions, environment, and history. When designing floral arrangements, my foremost inspiration is color. I look to nature, fashion, and art—to name a few inspiring subjects—for color combinations that appeal to me. I then translate these color concepts into compact floral arrangements in a way that the colors and textures will reveal themselves over time, like a great novel in which you find something new with every pass. I believe each arrangement can be, and should be, equally refreshing at every glance and should create interest with every subtle change in light or shadow. On a deeper level, arrangements should reveal something about the designer, such as the mood in which the arrangement was created. The terms used to describe the array—playful or dramatic, wistful or romantic—will reflect the intent of the designer. Floral arranging is such a cathartic and reflective creative process. I encourage others to tell their own stories, as I tell mine every day, through floral design.

Arturo Quintero

PRUDENCE DESIGNS

The Principles of Design

The initial choice of flowers is the single most important step in the flower-arranging process. Start with an idea of the type of arrangement you want to create—woodsy, loose and airy, summery, or an eclectic mix of your own design. Each design style will suggest certain types of flowers and they, in turn, will inspire ways to assemble them.

Size is an important consideration when arranging flowers. Using different-sized flowers in an arrangement creates dynamic visual interest. Generally, use larger flowers first, and work down to smaller accent flowers as in **"Sterling Pink"** (right) and **"French Harvest"** (opposite). For mound-shape arrangements, keep the tallest point in the center such as in the demure **"Little Black Dress"** (below).

Knowing the occasion for which you're preparing the arrangement is an integral part of the design process. For what occasion do you intend to display or present your arrangement? Is it a token of thanks, which might suggest a smaller, more compact arrangement? Or is it to celebrate the arrival of spring or to inspire thoughts of warm weather during the winter months? Perhaps the arrangement is a festive gesture marking the winter holidays. Your motives in creating the arrangements will help direct your choice and arrangement of the floral elements.

Setting also plays an important role in the creation of a floral arrangement. In which room will the arrangement be placed? **"Meadow in a Box"** (below) would look cheerful on a kitchen windowsill or country table.

"Sunny Side" (top left) might stand on the floor; "Spring Parade" (top right) might accent a powder room; "Special Occasion" (above) might be perfect for a bedroom side-table; and single elements from "Autumn Sun" (right) might provide just the right hint of color anywhere. Important questions are: Will the arrangement be against a wall? Is it a solid color or patterned? Will the arrangement be viewed from all sides, or only seen from one viewpoint? What is the style in the room? In a classically decorated room, elegant arrangements look at home; in a minimalist environment, a single bloom may make the boldest statement.

Color transforms our surroundings and influences our moods; it can reflect our personality and our taste. Don't be afraid to use color. Look to art for inspiration and color direction. To fully appreciate and use color, it is necessary to be familiar with color theory. Each primary color (red, blue, and yellow) has a secondary color (green, orange, and purple) directly opposite it on the color wheel. Because the secondary color enhances the primary color, secondary colors are also known as complements of each other. When primary and secondary colors are mixed, all of the resulting colors create a series of color schemes that are called monochromatic, analogous, tertiary, clash, or complimentary. **"Sunny Side"** (on page 54), with poppies in red, yellow, and

orange, is an example of an analogous arrangement. **"Lemonade"** (left) is an example of a monochromatic arrangement that features one color, yellow, and several of its tints.

Textural interest can be created by mixing flowers of different kinds and at varying stages of development. The natural texture of flowers, such as the feathery edge of parrot tulips, the velvety smooth surface of rose petals, and the frothy texture of hydrangea, can establish a textural dynamic that creates depth. Using multiple kinds of foliage can also create a pleasing combination of texture and color. **"Citrus Grove"** (top right) uses lemon leaves and hypericum leaves; **"Autumn Leaves"** (right) uses maple and oak. Using an odd number of stems in an arrangement also creates an interesting shift in focus. Consider mixing leaves of different shapes in different shades of green in one arrangement for a more subtle effect.

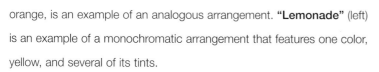

The container is critical to the overall proportion of the arrangement. Anything that can hold the foam is considered a container. The most important elements when working with proportion are the scale of the flowers in relationship to the container and the scale of the arrangement in relation to its purpose and placement. Use your imagination to make an impact with your arrangement—it's better to go overboard than to be unnoticed.

Many basic configurations in flower arranging are taken from geometry: round, triangular, and square. These shapes can be established in the arrangement overall, or they can be juxtaposed within one arrangement to create dynamic movement and a pleasing shift in focal point. The rounded mound shape is one of our favorites, as seen in **"Fuchsia Fiesta"** and **"First Blush"** (opposite far left). To achieve a modern look, keep the flowers in this dome shape tightly packed. The triangular shape can be seen in **"Welcome Wreath."** When mixing shapes within an arrangement, consider placing large flowers at the "corners" of a square, slightly smaller flowers at points of a triangle, and medium-headed flowers and berry clusters in the center of the arrangement, as in **"Sweet Charlotte"** (below). Asymmetry is another favorite design concept, and it can be applied simply by placing the floral elements in an off-balance way. Also, remember to: work with in-season flowers; allow blossoms to fall below the container's rim; and bend stems to mimic their natural curve—all measures to create a convincingly real design.

Remembering and practicing all of the principles above will ensure a beautiful, organic-looking arrangement.

Mixing Shapes

Use shape to establish a dynamic design by viewing the arrangement from above.

 Hot-pink roses form an upright triangle.

 Light-pink lilies form an inverted triangle.

 Pink daisies oppose one another, as do light-pink roses.

Spring

In this time of **renewal** and **rebirth,** let the flowers of the season awaken you from the dark days of winter with their **fresh colors** and **sweet fragrances.** Be inspired by **Nature,** and flatter her with imitation.

First Blush

MATERIALS
20 small roses, light pink,
   with foliage in dark
   green
20 stems of rose foliage
   (cut from rose stems),
   each with 3–5 leaves
Styrofoam
Ceramic vase, opalescent
   green, 6" (15.2cm) high
   with a 5"-dia. (12.7cm)
   lip and a 2½-dia.
   (6.2cm) base

TOOLS
Serrated knife
Cutting board
Ruler
Wire cutters

A loose, "unstructured" gathering of beautiful roses

in a blush color brings the freshness of late spring into

your home. Adding to the "just-picked" look are the

sprays of leafy stems that extend above the flower

heads, evoking the look of roses growing in a garden.

Placed in a simple ceramic vase, so as not to distract

the eye from the unencumbered beauty of the blooms,

"First Blush" is the perfect accent for a bedside table or

a console, but its fresh sensibility will make any room

feel new and revitalized.

If the rose stems and the leafy stems are not stiff enough to be inserted easily into the foam, consider substituting softer floral foam for the Styrofoam.

CREATING "FIRST BLUSH"

1 Lay the Styrofoam on the cutting board, and trim it to fit inside the vase using the serrated knife. Insert the foam into the vase so that it fits snugly and rests ½–¾ in. (1.3–2cm) below the lip of the container.

2 Use the wire cutters to cut each leafy stem to 6 in. (15.2cm). Insert the stems into the foam, building a loose mound-shape with a high center.

3 Use the wire cutters to cut each rose stem to 6 in. (15.2cm). Begin inserting the stems of a few roses in the center of the foam, clustering the floral heads together as shown.

4 Insert the remaining rose stems into the foam, clustering them around the blooms inserted in step 3 to form a tightly-packed mound shape.

Lemonade

MATERIALS

4 cymbidium orchid stems
  with 1 blossom each,
  yellow
1 cymbidium orchid stem
  with 1 blossom and 2
  buds, yellow
2 large leucospermum,
  yellow
8 small Styrofoam lemons,
  2" wide x 3" long (5cm
  x 7⅗cm)
1 stem of lemon leaves,
  dark green, each with 5
  branches and 3–5
  leaves on each branch
5 medium ranunculus,
  orange
5 medium ranunculus,
  yellow
4 small ranunculus, yellow
3 small roses, yellow
13 floral picks
Floral tape
Styrofoam
Water pitcher with handle
  and spout, chartreuse,
  6½" high (12.7cm) with
  a 5"-dia. (15.2cm) rim

TOOLS

Serrated knife
Cutting board
Ruler
Wire cutters
Awl

A simple chartreuse-green pitch-

er overflows with an exuberant

gathering of sunny lemon-yellow

flowers and plump fruit. Arranged in a dome shape, the

velvet texture of the flowers contrasts nicely with the pol-

ished glaze on the pitcher. Packing the flowers tightly in

the container, and allowing some blooms to cascade

over its rim, transforms a small arrangement into a bold

focal point. Ideal for a breakfast area or sunroom, this

arrangement will add a cheerful accent to any room.

"*A bit of fragrance clings to the hand that gives flowers.*"

———

Chinese Proverb

CREATING "LEMONADE"

1 Lay the Styrofoam on the cutting board, and cut it to fit within the pitcher using a serrated knife. Insert the foam into the pitcher so that it fits snugly and rests ½–¾ in. (1.3–2cm) below the rim of the pitcher.

2 Use the wire cutters to trim the stems of all five orchids to 6 in. (15.2cm). Insert two stems into the foam at the front right side of the pitcher so that the blossoms hang over the rim. Insert a stem of orchids with buds at the back right side, another at the back left side, and the remaining orchid at the front left side.

3 Use the wire cutters to trim the stems of leucospermum to 6 in. (15.2cm). Insert one stem into the foam in the center of the arrangement, angling it toward the back. Insert the second stem in the center, angling it toward the front.

4 Secure each lemon using a floral pick. Use wire cutters to trim the picks to 6 in. (15.2cm). Insert the picked lemons into the foam, arranging them randomly throughout the flowers.

5 Secure each branch of lemon leaves using a floral pick, if necessary. Use wire cutters to trim the picks to 6 in. (15.2cm). Insert the picked leaves into the foam, arranging them randomly throughout the flowers and lemons.

6 Use wire cutters to trim the stems of the ranunculus and the roses to 6 in. (15.2cm). Use them to fill in any remaining spaces, or "holes," in the arrangement. 🖉

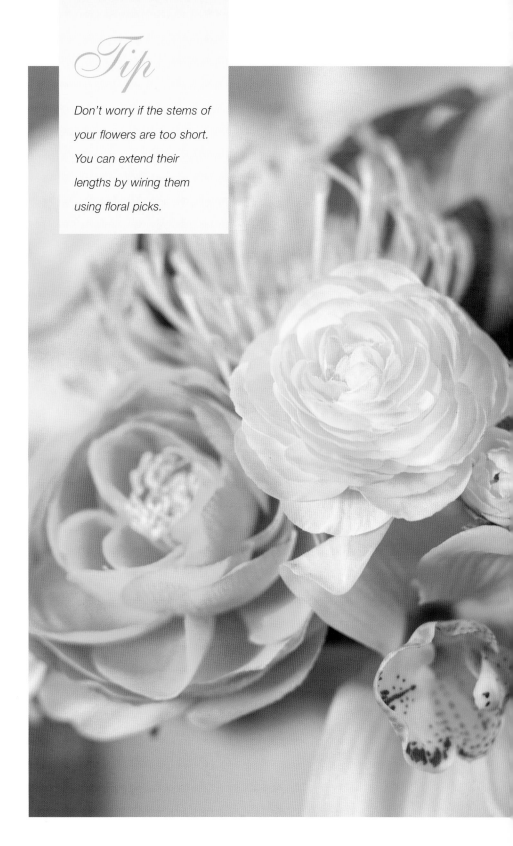

Tip

Don't worry if the stems of your flowers are too short. You can extend their lengths by wiring them using floral picks.

Simply Modern

MATERIALS
1 large banana leaf, green,
  22" (55.8cm) long and
  4" (10.2cm) wide
1 large hydrangea, white,
  with leaves
2 large parrot tulips, white
1 small allium, white
8 small viburnum, green,
  with foliage
6 ranunculus, white, with
  buds and foliage
2 anemones, white, with
  leaves
4 nigellas, white, with
  foliage
Styrofoam
Glass vase, 5"-cube
  (12.7cm)

TOOLS
Serrated knife
Cutting board
Ruler
Floral pins
Wire cutters

Reminiscent of those enlivening first buds of springtime,

this fresh-as-outdoors arrangement is made by combin-

ing flowers and foliage in the palest of spring greens and

bright white. By limiting the colorway of the floral material,

the texture of each of the floral elements becomes the

focus of the dome-shaped design.

CREATING "SIMPLY MODERN"

1 Lay a block of Styrofoam on a cutting board, and cut it to fit within the glass vase using the serrated knife. Wrap and secure a banana leaf around the foam, following the directions on page 182. Insert the wrapped-foam block into the glass vase.

2 Use wire cutters to trim the stems of the hydrangeas and the tulips to 6 in. (15.2 cm). Insert the hydrangea stem into the foam at the front right corner of the vase so that it hangs over the rim. Insert the stems of both tulips into the foam at the back left corner of the vase.

3 Use wire cutters to trim the stem of the white allium to 6 in. (15.2 cm). Insert the stem into the foam at the front left corner of the vase.

4 Use wire cutters to trim the stems of the green viburnums to 6 in. (15.2 cm). Insert the stems into the foam, spacing them throughout the center of the arrangement. Note: Begin at the front of the arrangement between the viburnum and the hydrangea, and work toward the back.

5 Use wire cutters to trim the stems of the ranunculus, the buds, and the anemones to 6 in. (15.2 cm). Insert the stems of the ranunculus and the buds into the foam, distributing them throughout the arrangement. Insert the stem of one anemone at the right side with one bloom facing toward the front and the other facing toward the back.

6 Use wire cutters to trim the stems of the nigellas to 6 in. (15.2 cm). Insert the nigella stems into the foam to fill in any remaining spaces, or "holes." ✐

Tip

If finding one leaf that
is long enough to cover
the Styrofoam is proving
difficult, use two leaves
of equal width to line
the vase.

Special Occasion

ESSENTIALS

How to Prepare a
  Container (See page
  176.)
How to Cut a Wire Stem
(See page 178.)

MATERIALS

6 large roses, pink, with
  foliage
1 medium hydrangea,
  white, with foliage
2 medium roses, white
10 small pompons, white,
  with foliage
4 small viburnum, green,
  with foliage
1 Stargazer lily, with bud
3 stems of hypericum
  foliage with berries, dark
  green, with 2 branches
  and 6–9 leaves on each
  branch
2 small ranunculus, hot
  pink
Stem of jasmine vines,
  dark pink, with 4 vines
Styrofoam
Slender bronze loving cup,
  9" (22.9cm) high with a
  5¼"-dia. (13.3cm) rim

TOOLS

Serrated knife
Cutting board
Ruler
Wire cutters

Elegant and formal, "Special Occasion" is suited to

events such as a special anniversary or a wedding

reception at home. The sophisticated arrangement of

white and pink flowers is accented by a pair of blooms in

hot pink. The billowing floral mound appears to blossom

above the rim of a burnished bronze loving cup, evoking

the paintings of the Old Dutch Masters.

Traditional in style, the arrangement can

be placed on an entry table to

welcome your guests.

CREATING "SPECIAL OCCASION"

1 Lay the Styrofoam on a cutting board, and cut it to fit within the loving cup using the serrated knife. Insert the foam into the cup so that it fits snugly and rests ½–¾ in. (1.3–2cm) below the rim of the container.

2 Use wire cutters to trim the stems of the pink roses to 7 in. (17.8cm). Insert the rose stems into the foam in the front of the arrangement, one at a time, to create a wavy line.

3 Use wire cutters to trim the stems of the white hydrangea and the roses to 7 in. (17.8cm). Insert the stem of the hydrangea into the foam at the front right side of the arrangement. Insert one white rose behind the hydrangea and the second at the back right side of the arrangement.

4 Use wire cutters to trim the stems of the pompons to 7 in. (17.8cm). Gather three stems into a cluster, and insert them into the foam in the center of the front side of the arrangement. Insert the remaining stems of pompoms in two- and three-bloom clusters throughout the arrangement.

5 Use wire cutters to trim the stems of the viburnum to 7 in. (17.8cm). Insert one stem into the foam at the left front side of the arrangement and a second stem in the center. Distribute the remaining viburnum stems throughout the arrangement.

6 Use wire cutters to trim the stem of the lily bud and the lily to 7 in. (17.8cm). Insert the stem of the bud into the foam in the center of the arrangement. Then insert the stem of the lily toward the back left side of the arrangement.

(continued on the next page)

7 Use wire cutters to trim the stems of the hypericum leaf and the ranunculus to 9 in. (22.9cm). Distribute the leaves evenly throughout the arrangement. Insert the stem of the hot-pink ranunculus into the foam in the center of the arrangement.

8 Use wire cutters to trim each jasmine vine to 10 in. (25.4cm). Insert the vines into the arrangement, distributing them evenly throughout the flowers. Allow the vines to extend beyond the perimeter of the arrangement 1–2 in. (2.5cm–5cm).

"Blossom by blossom the spring begins."
— A. Swinburn

Tip

To add an element of surprise in an all-pastel arrangement, position a few small blooms in a bright color in a prominent place among the other floral elements.

Citrus Grove

MATERIALS

20 large foam lemons, 4"
(10.2 cm) long with a
2½"-dia. (6.3cm)

12 stems of lemon foliage,
dark green, each with 5
branches and 7–9
leaves on each branch

7 stems of hypericum
leaves, dark green, with
berries, each with 2
branches and 6–9
leaves on each branch

Floral foam

20 floral picks

Metal container, lime
green, with wicker frame
in white metal, 6½" wide
x 6" high x 6½" deep
(16.5cm x 15.2cm
x 16.5cm)

TOOLS

Serrated knife

Cutting board

Ruler

Wire cutters

Hot-glue gun and
glue sticks

Awl

A mound of bright-yellow lemons and green lemon leaves are arranged in a lime green container, creating a lively design that will add a cheerful note of freshness to any environment. The lemons are nestled liberally among the green leaves in a way that imitates the way they look when fruit-laden branches are just cut from the tree. One of the secrets to creating a successful arrangement is to avoid having the arrangement look contrived. For an organic appearance, look to nature for inspiration, and keep the arrangement simple for bold impact.

Tip

When using flowers or leaves that don't have supportive wire stems, attach floral picks to the stems to give them more support. If the majority of stems require picks to reinforce them, substitute more malleable floral foam for hard Styrofoam for easier insertion.

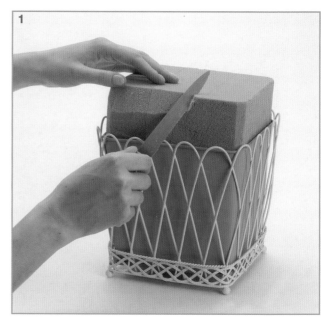

" *What sunshine is to flowers, smiles are to humanity.*"

—*Joseph Addison*

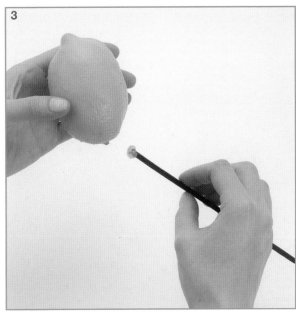

CREATING "CITRUS GROVE"

1 Lay the floral foam on a cutting board, and cut the foam to fit within the container using a serrated knife. Firmly push the trimmed foam into the container so that it fits snugly and protrudes 3 in. (7.6cm) above the rim of the container. Use the knife to shave off the corners of the foam to form a mound, as shown.

2 Use the wire cutters to cut all stems. Trim the lemon and hypericum branches to 8 in. (20.3cm). Insert the stems into the foam in a random fashion to create a loose mound of leaves, with the highest point in the center.

3 Follow the directions on page 180 to attach one floral pick to each lemon. Use the wire cutters to shorten their lengths, if needed, to achieve the desired effect when inserting them in the next step.

4 Insert each picked lemon into the foam, distributing the lemons evenly throughout the arrangement. 🖋

Spring Parade

MATERIALS

1 large galax leaf, dark
   green
2 large hydrangeas, blue,
   with foliage in dark
   green
2 large hydrangea leaves
   (cut from hydrangea
   stems)
1 large peony, pink, with
   leaves
1 medium rose, pink, with
   leaves
6 irises, purple
4 stems of hypericum
   foliage with berries,
   each with 2 branches
   and 5–6 leaves on each
   branch
Styrofoam
Wooden box, 6½" wide
   x 5" high x x 6½" deep
   (16.5cm x 12.7cm
   x 16.5cm)

TOOLS

Serrated knife
Cutting board
Ruler
Wire cutters

Like a garden in bloom that is transplanted indoors, the flowers in this charming wooden box look as if they were gathered at random. The appeal of the romantic combination of a wooden box and the simple garden blooms is their simplicity. The leaves form the base of the arrangement, and the blossoms seem to spring up in the center, keeping the arrangement looking natural. Ideal for a coffee table, "Spring Parade" will add a breath of spring to any room.

CREATING "SPRING PARADE"

1 Lay the Styrofoam on the cutting board, and cut it to fit within the box using a serrated knife. Insert the trimmed foam into the box using firm pressure until it fits snugly and rests ½ in.–¾ in. (1.3cm–2cm) below the lip.

2 Use the wire cutters to trim all three-leaf stems to 4 in. (10.2cm). Insert the stem of the galax leaf into the foam in the front right corner of the box so that it hangs over the edge. Insert one hydrangea leaf stem into the front left corner and the second into the back left corner. Let both hang over the edge.

3 Use the wire cutters to trim the hydrangea stems to 6 in. (15.2cm). Insert each stem into the foam at the back right corner.

4 Use the wire cutters to trim the stems of the rose and the peony to 6 in. (15.2cm). Insert the rose stem into the foam at the front right corner just above the galax leaf. Insert the peony stem into the foam in the center of the arrangement.

5 Use the wire cutters to trim the stems of the irises to 6 in. (15.2cm). Insert four stems into the foam beginning at the back left corner and ending at the front right corner of the arrangement. Insert the remaining two irises toward the front left corner.

6 Use the wire cutters to cut the hypericum branches to 6 in. (15.2cm). Insert them into the arrangement to fill the remaining spaces, or "holes."

Tip

To create a lush arrangement that requires little money and time to make, use floral materials with large-scale elements, such as large flowers and leaves.

" Unity and simplicity are the two sources of beauty."

—J. J. Winckelmann

MATERIALS

1 medium hydrangea,
white, with foliage

1 large hydrangea, white,
with foliage in dark
green

2 large hydrangea leaves
(cut from large
hydrangea stem)

1 Casablanca Lily stem,
with two blossoms,
white

1 Casablanca Lily stem,
with one blossom and
two buds, white

3 medium roses, white,
with foliage in dark
green

3 stems of rose foliage
(cut from rose stems),
each with 3–5 leaves

1 stem small hydrangeas,
white, with foliage and
5 blossoms

Chopsticks

Styrofoam

Chinese food container in
lime green, 4¼" wide
x 4½" high x 3¼" deep
(10.6cm x 11.4cm
x 8.2cm)

TOOLS

Serrated knife

Cutting board

Ruler

Wire cutters

Spring Joy

This novel approach to flower

arranging—using a Chinese

take-out carton as a floral

container—typifies the kind of arrangement that

gets noticed wherever it is displayed. Consistent with

the Asian-inspired design are the chopsticks, which are

placed off-center, adding an amusing note to the witty

little arrangement. Quick and easy to put together, make

several "Spring Joy" arrangements to accent a buffet

table, where they'll look good enough to eat.

Tip

Experiment using other unique containers, like a Pyrex measuring cup, with its red demarcation lines, or several antique perfume bottles. The larger the container is, the more floral material that will be required to create an arrangement with impact.

CREATING "SPRING JOY"

1 Lay the Styrofoam on a cutting board, and cut it to fit within the take-out carton using a serrated knife. Using firm pressure, insert the foam into the carton so that it fits snugly and sits ½ in.–¾ in. (1.3cm–2cm) below the lip of the carton.

2 Use the wire cutters to trim the stems of the hydrangea leaves to 4 in. (10.2cm). Insert the stems into the foam at the front right corner of the carton so that the leaves hang over the edge of the carton.

3 Use the wire cutters to trim the stems of the large and medium hydrangeas to 5 in. (12.7cm). Insert the stems of the medium-size hydrangea into the foam in the center of the right side of the arrangement. Angle the head of the bloom toward the back right corner. Insert the stem of the large-size hydrangea into the foam at the back left corner.

4 Use the wire cutters to trim the stem of the lily with two blossoms to 5 in. (12.7cm). Insert the stem into the foam in the center front of the arrangement. *(continued on page 51)*

"*The Earth laughs
in flowers.*"

—*Ralph Waldo
Emerson*

5 Use the wire cutters to trim the stem of the lily with buds to 5 in. (12.7cm). Insert the stem into the foam at the back right corner.

6 Use the wire cutters to trim the stems of the roses to 5 in. (12.7cm). Insert one stem into the foam at the front right corner, a second at the front left corner, and a third at the back right corner.

7 Use the wire cutters to trim the stems of the small-size hydrangea and the stems of rose leaves to 5 in. (12.7cm). Use them to fill in any remaining spaces, or "holes," within the arrangement.

8 To finish, insert the chop-sticks into the arrangement at an angle, as shown. 🍃

Tip

If you are giving a luncheon, create mul-tiples of the "Spring Joy" design. Set one at each place setting, and you have instant favors for your guests.

Bright summer days spent basking in the warmth of the **sun** inspired these designs, which include everything from cool **tropical** elements to **saturated colors** extracted from Latin cultures. Even the all-white arrangement will look **fresh** long after Labor Day.

Summer

Sunny Side

MATERIALS

8 poppies with buds,
red, with foliage
3 poppies with buds,
yellow, with foliage
2 poppies with buds,
orange, with foliage
2 poppies with buds, red
and orange, with foliage
Sheet moss, green
Floral pins
Styrofoam
Galvanized flower bucket,
11" (27.9cm) high with a
6"-dia. (15.2cm) rim and
a 4"-dia. (10cm) base

TOOLS

Serrated knife
Cutting board
Ruler
Wire cutters

A whimsical arrangement of poppies in tomato red, butter yellow, and red-orange are informally arranged in a galvanized bucket, creating the look of just-picked wild flowers at the market. The secret to creating the airy look of the arrangement is the wired stems of the poppies that can be bent to change the direction of the blooms, imitating the look of naturally-growing flowers. Taking little time to arrange, "Sunny Side" is a great way to add vibrant energy and color to any corner in your home.

In nature, poppy stems are very weak before the flower heads develop and the stems thicken. For the most life-like appearance in a faux flower arrangement, the stems of the buds should be bent so that they arch and curve as shown at left.

1

2

3

CREATING "SUNNY SIDE"

1 Place the Styrofoam on the cutting board, and use the serrated knife to trim it to snugly fit inside the flower bucket. Insert the foam into the bucket so it rests ½ in.– ¾ in. (1.3cm–1.9cm) below the rim.

2 Use wire cutters to cut all stems. Trim the red poppy stems to 20 in. (50.8cm). Insert the stems into the foam randomly.

3 Cut the yellow, orange, and red-and-orange poppies to 20 in. (50.8cm). Insert the stems, distributing the colors evenly throughout. Vary the height of the flowers slightly, with the tallest flowers at the center. Bend the stems as shown, allowing the flowers to face outward from the center.

4 Tuck the moss around the base of the arrangement to conceal the foam, securing the moss in place using floral pins. ✐

Little Black Dress

ESSENTIALS
How to Prepare a
   Container (See page
   176.)
How to Cut a Wire Stem
   (See page 178.)

MATERIALS
15 garden roses, hot pink,
   with foliage
Styrofoam
Glass vase, black, 2" wide
   x 4" high x 2" deep
   (5cm x 10cm x 5cm)

TOOLS
Serrated knife
Cutting board
Ruler
Wire cutters

Flower arrangements don't need to be complicated to be

beautiful. In fact, this small, sensual arrangement of gar-

den roses inspires romance and excitement because of

its simplicity—hot-pink roses are clustered in a simple

black glass vase that adds drama and frames the

blossoms to great effect. The

arrangement can work well in

a simple, modern interior or in

a traditional interior that has more

intricate patterns and textures.

4

CREATING "LITTLE BLACK DRESS"

1 Place the Styrofoam on the cutting board, and use the serrated knife to trim it to fit snugly inside the vase. Insert the foam into the vase so it rests ½ in.–¾ in. (1.3cm–2cm) below the rim.

2 Use the wire cutters to trim the rose stems to 4 in. (10cm). Insert the stems into the foam around the rim of the vase, placing the blooms as close together as possible. Bend the stems so the blooms face out and slightly down.

3 Insert the rest of the roses into the center of the arrangement, creating a tight mound with the highest point in the center. Bend the faces of the flowers at the center of the arrangement upward.

4 Reach between the roses, and position the foliage so it extends beyond the blooms.

Tip

This arrangement is so easy to make, you'll want to create multiples to line up on a mantle or along the center of a dining room table.

Meadow in a Box

A cheerful accent on a kitchen windowsill or a charming decorative accent on a buffet table, "Meadow in a Box" brings the natural look of a flowering meadow inside. Placed in a rectangular metal box with a gleaming silver finish, the simple arrangement has a breezy quality reinforced by the random placement of the flowers in the grassy "field" and the uneven heights of the flower heads.

ESSENTIALS

- How to Prepare a Container (See page 176.)
- How to Cut a Wire Stem (See page 178.)

MATERIALS

- Artificial grass, green, 10" x 10" (25.4cm x 25.4cm) slab
- 12 cosmos with buds, orange, with foliage
- Floral pins
- Styrofoam
- Metal window box, silver-tone, 14" wide x 3" high x 5" deep x (35.6cm x 7.6cm x 12.7cm)

TOOLS

- Serrated knife
- Cutting board
- Ruler
- Wire cutters

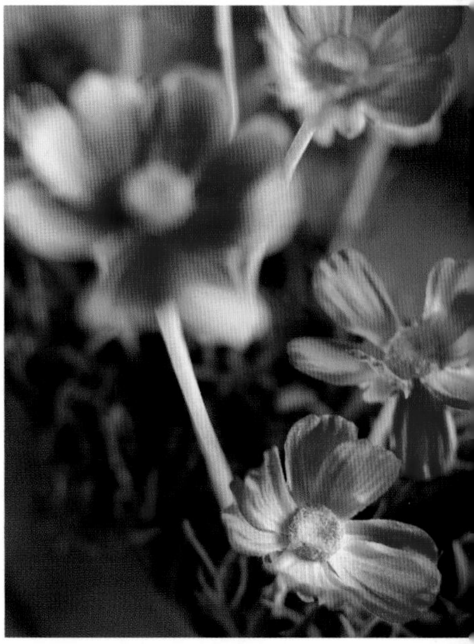

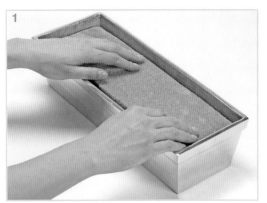

Tip

Window boxes are a wonderful addition to any room, but they really brighten up the kitchen. In addition to cosmos, try other flowers such as lavender, anemone, daisy, or bachelor's button.

CREATING "MEADOW IN A BOX"

1 Place the Styrofoam on the cutting board, and use the serrated knife to trim it to fit snugly inside the window box. Insert the foam into the window box so it rests ½ in. – ¾ in. (1.3cm–2cm) below the rim.

2 Use the wire cutters to cut the grass into two 5-in. x 10-in. (12.7cm x 25.4cm) rectangles. Set one rectangle aside. Cut a 5-in. x 4-in. (12.7cm x 10cm) piece from the second rectangle. Trim off any unnecessary plastic. Set the remainder aside for another use.

3 Place the large grass rectangle on the foam at the left side of the window box. Position the small rectangle to the right of the first piece, and butt the edges. Secure the grass using a floral pin at each corner.

4 Use the wire cutters to cut the four cosmos with buds to 11 in. (27.9cm), and the rest to 8 in. (20.3cm). Insert the cosmos stems through the grass and into the foam. Space the flowers as shown, varying their heights and curving the stems for a natural look. ✐

Sweet Charlotte

MATERIALS

2 fern fiddleheads, green
1 wax flower stem, pink,
  with 4 branches
3 medium white-edged
  roses, hot pink, with
  foliage
2 daisies, pale pink
2 medium roses, pale
  pink, with foliage
3 lilies, pale pink
2 garden roses, hot pink,
  with foliage
2 large galax leaves, dark
  green
2 large hydrangea leaves,
  dark green
24-gauge floral wire
Floral tape, medium green
3 yds. (2.8m) of 1"-wide
  (2.5cm) grosgrain
  ribbon, brown

MATERIALS

Ruler
Wire cutters
Scissors
Hot-glue gun and
  glue sticks

Gathering flowers to make a bouquet has been practiced for centuries. Whether a few stems of wildflowers or an exuberant cluster of hothouse flowers, bouquets are treasured for their sentimentality and their decorative value. Here, flowers in soft pink and cream are clustered together with fern fiddleheads, adding a note of whimsy. A ribbon in rich chocolate brown wraps around the stems to secure them, and streamers cascade below.

Tip

A bouquet is a tight mound of flowers with the highest point in the center, the same as if it were created in a vase.

CREATING "SWEET CHARLOTTE"

1 See "Gathering the Flowers" on page 69 for instructions on how to arrange the blooms. Use wire cutters to cut all of the stems to 12 in. (30.5cm) so they are easier to manage. When the flowers are arranged, cut the stems to 6 in. (15.2cm). Secure the stems together using floral wire and then floral tape.

2 Use wire cutters to trim the bottom of the stems even.

3 Use the scissors to cut the ribbon in half. Set one half aside. Using the other half of the ribbon, apply a drop of glue to one side of a ribbon end, and adhere it to the bottom of the stems. Working from the stem ends upward, tightly wrap the ribbon around the stems, lapping each wrap over the previous one. Trim away the excess ribbon, and secure the ribbon end using a drop of glue at the base of the flowers.

4 Wrap the second half of ribbon around the base of the flowers, over the glued, raw ribbon end, and tie it into a bow. Secure the bow to the stems using a drop of glue.

Gathering the Flowers

Cut the wax flower stem into four branches. Starting in the center, gather the flowers in the following order: fiddleheads, wax flower branches, white roses with hot-pink edges, daisies, pale pink roses, lilies, hot-pink roses, galax leaves, and hydrangea leaves.

Beach House

MATERIALS

2 large hydrangeas, white,
   with foliage
2 large hydrangeas, green,
   with foliage
8 large hydrangea leaves
   (cut from hydrangea
   stems)
3 large peonies, white,
   with foliage
2 magnolias, white, with
   foliage
4 medium roses, pale
   green, with foliage
8 narcissus, paper white,
   with foliage
2 stems of any kind, light
   green, with buds
1 stem of myrtle, dark
   green, with 2 branches
Styrofoam
Ceramic planter, char-
   treuse, 7" (17.8cm)
   high, with a 7"-dia.
   (17.8cm) rim and a
   5"-dia. (12.7cm) base

TOOLS

Serrated knife
Cutting board
Ruler
Wire cutters

Inspired by a beach cottage—bleached colors, sun

streaming through windows, white linens, and shore

breezes–this nearly all-white arrangement features flowers

that grow reliably summer after summer: roses,

hydrangea, and peonies, bringing back memories of

relaxed summer days. Arranged loosely

in a footed vase, some of the

blooms fall over slightly,

imitating their natural

growth in a summer garden.

" Arranging flowers ...can give a sense of quiet in a crowded day..."
—Anne Morrow Lindbergh

1

2

CREATING "BEACH HOUSE"

1 Place the Styrofoam on the cutting board, and use the serrated knife to trim it to fit snugly inside the planter. Insert the foam into the planter so it rests ½ in.–¾ in. (1.3cm–1.9cm) below the rim.

2 Use wire cutters to cut all stems. Trim the hydrangea leaf stems to 4 in. (10.2cm). Insert the stems into the foam around the rim of the planter.

3 Cut the white hydrangea stems to 8 in. (20.3cm). Insert one stem into the back left side and the second into the front right side. Curve the stems so the blooms face outward and slightly down.

4 Trim the green hydrangea stems to 8 in. (20.3cm). Insert one stem into the front left side and the second into the back right side. Curve the stems so the blooms face outward and slightly down.
(continued on the next page)

Tip

Instead of presenting a floral arrangement as a single design element, arrange a tableau of decorative elements, such as boxes and biblots in contrasting materials, to add ecclectic style.

3

4

5 Cut the peony stems to 8 in. (20.3cm). Insert two peonies into the center of the arrangement. Insert the third peony into the right side between the white and green hydrangea.

6 Trim the magnolia stems to 8 in. (20.3cm). Insert one magnolia into the center back. Insert the second into the center front.

7 Cut the rose and paper white stems to 10 in. (25.4cm). Insert them to fill any remaining spaces.

8 Trim the light-green stems and myrtle branches to 10 in. (25.4cm). Insert one light-green stem into the center, and the other stem into the right side. Have them extend 3–4 in. (7.6–10.2cm) above the arrangement. Insert the myrtle stems into the front right side, curving them so they trail downward to the base of the planter.

" Flowers carry on dialogues with [Nature] through the graceful bending of their stems…"
—Auguste Rodin

Sterling Pink

MATERIALS

2 stems of lemon foliage,
  dark green, each with 5
  branches and 7 leaves
  on each branch
3 large peonies, pink, with
  foliage
2 large hydrangeas, pink,
  with foliage
2 small hydrangeas, pink
  and green, with foliage
3 Stargazer lilies, pink,
  with foliage, one with
  2 buds
10 small roses, pink
Styrofoam
Urn, silvertone,
  7" (17.8cm) high with a
  7"-dia. (17.8cm) rim, a
  5"-dia. (12.7cm) bowl,
  and a 4" dia. (7.6cm)
  base

TOOLS

Serrated knife
Cutting board
Ruler
Wire cutters

Full-blown peonies,

hydrangeas, and lilies that range in color

from the palest pink to lush rose and cerise-tinged blush fill

a footed silver urn in a modified loving-cup shape. The

contrasting textures of the flowers—a mix of "embossed,"

frilly, and velvety surfaces—provide a nice counterpoint to

the highly-polished surface of the antique silver container.

Flowers in shades of pink always bring a sense of fresh-

ness to an arrangement and the rooms into which they are

placed, making them a favorite choice of floral designers.

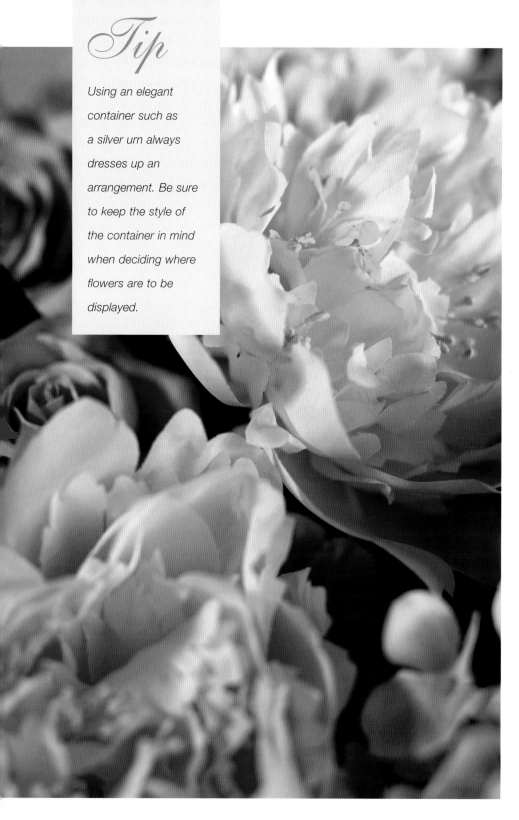

CREATING "STERLING PINK"

1 Place the Styrofoam on the cutting board, and use the serrated knife to trim it to fit snugly inside the urn. Insert the foam into the urn so it rests ½ in.–¾ in. (1.3cm–1.9cm) below the rim.

2 Use wire cutters to cut all stems. Trim each lemon-leaf branch to 12 in. (30.5cm). Insert the leaves into the foam, creating a loose mound, with the highest point in the center.

3 Cut the peony stems to 10 in. (25.4cm). Insert one peony stem into the center of the arrangement with the flower facing upward. Insert the second and third peonies at the left and right, just above the rim of the urn. Have the flowers facing outward and slightly down.

4 Trim the hydrangea stems to 10 in. (25.4cm). Insert one large hydrangea stem into the back on the left side of the arrangement. Insert the second large hydrangea stem into the back on the right side. Insert the small hydrangea stems randomly into the arrangement.

5 Cut the lilies to 10 in. (25.4cm). Set the lily with the buds aside. Insert one lily into the left side of the arrangement. Insert the second lily into the right side. Insert the lily with the buds into the center of the arrangement. Allow the buds to extend 1 in.–2 in. (2.5cm –5.1cm) above the other flowers.

6 Trim the roses to 10 in. (25.4cm). Insert them into the arrangement to fill the remaining spaces or "holes." ✑

Sterling Pink **79**

Tropical Paradise

MATERIALS

1 extra-large banana leaf,
   9" x 24" (22.9cm x
   61cm) plus the stem
1 extra-large split-leaf
   philodendron, 16" x 15"
   (40.6cm x 38cm) plus
   the stem
1 cymbidium orchid stem,
   with 7 blooms and 2
   buds, chartreuse, 17"
   (43.2cm) long plus
   the stem
2 ginger pod stems,
   green, each pod 3" x 5"
   (7.6cm x 12.7cm)
2 curly willows, 26"
   (66cm) long
Spanish moss
Floral pins
Styrofoam
Wooden box, 8" wide
   x 9" high x 4" deep
   (20.3cm x 22.9cm
   x 10.2cm)

TOOLS

Serrated knife
Cutting board
Ruler
Wire cutters

Evoke the feel of an exotic rain forest, and add a vibrant

splash of natural color to any interior space in your home

with this dramatic floral design.

Composed of a rustic wooden

box, bold-sized leaves, and

delicate orchids, the mix of

elements in "Tropical Paradise"

adds a sense of architecture to

the arrangement while retaining

its natural style sensibility.

CREATING "TROPICAL PARADISE"

1 Place the Styrofoam on the cutting board, and use the serrated knife to trim it to fit snugly inside the wooden box. Insert the foam into the box so it rests ½ in.–¾ in. (1.3cm–1.9cm) below the rim.

2 Use wire cutters to cut all stems. Trim the stem of the banana leaf to 7 in. (17.8cm). Insert the stem into the foam in the back right corner. Bend the leaf toward the right.

3 Cut the stem of the philodendron to 7 in. (17.8cm). Insert the stem into the front left corner, and bend the leaf toward the left.

4 Trim the stem of the orchid to 7 in. (17.8cm). Insert the stem into center front, and angle the flower portion of the stem toward the right.

5 Cut the ginger pods to 24 in. (61cm) overall. Insert the first ginger stem behind and left, and at the same height as the orchid stem. Insert the second ginger stem to the right of the first, behind and higher than the orchid stem.

6 Twist each length of curly willow into a loose corkscrew. Insert them into the center behind the ginger pods, angled toward the left. Have one the same height as the orchids, and the other 2 in. (5.1cm) higher than the topmost ginger pod. Tuck wads of moss around the base of the arrangement to conceal the foam. Allow some moss to hang over the edge of the box. Secure the moss using floral pins. ✐

Faux flowers look stiff and unnatural until their stems are manipulated into graceful curves. Then they seem to come alive.

"*Deep in their root, all flowers keep the light.*"
—*Theodore Roethke*

Fuchsia Fiesta

ESSENTIALS

How to Prepare a
 Container (See page
 176.)
How to Cut a Wire Stem
 (See page 178.)

MATERIALS

24 small ranunculus,
 fuchsia
20 extra small ranunculus,
 fuchsia, with foliage
Floral foam
Ceramic vase, opalescent
 green, 6" (15.2cm) high
 with a 5"-dia. (12.7cm)
 rim and a 2"-dia. (5cm)
 base

TOOLS

Serrated knife
Cutting board
Ruler
Wire cutters

A profusion of ranunculus in a rich fuchsia color is all

you need to create this simply elegant design. Crowded

loosely together to form a dome shape, the delicate flow-

ers are arranged in a glazed ceramic vase that has simple

lines; its slightly opalescent finish

reflects a warm glow and moves the

eye to the cluster of blooms, creat-

ing a party for the spirit. A few

buds "grow" above the flowers

as they might in a garden.

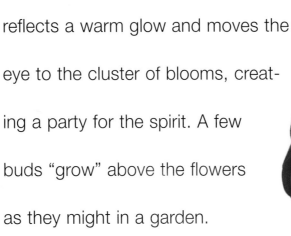

Tip   A monochromatic arrangement using only one type of flower is a fast and easy way to create a no-fail yet elegant floral design.

CREATING "FUCHSIA FIESTA"

1 Place the floral foam on the cutting board, and use the serrated knife to trim it to fit snugly inside the vase. Insert the foam into the vase so it rests ½ in.–¾ in. (1.3cm–1.9cm) below the rim.

2 Use the wire cutters to trim all ranunculus stems to 6 in. (15.2cm). Set three extra-small ranunculuses aside. Using a mixture of small and extra-small blooms, insert a row of stems into the foam around the rim of the vase. Bend the stems so they curve outward and the flowers face slightly downward. Have the petals touching.

3 Fill the center of the arrangement, building it up to create a tight mound, with the highest point in the center. Curve the stems so the flowers face outward, then upward, as shown. Allow the blooms to overlap, with some inserted further into the arrangement than others. Use all the ranunculus stems with the exception of three extra-small ones.

4 Insert the three extra-small stems into the center of the arrangement. Position the blooms above the other flowers so that ½ in.–2 in. (1.3cm–5.1cm) of their stems show. ✑

In this most **texturally appealing** and **richly colored** season, arrangements feature **burnt oranges** and **deep yellows,** augmented by colorful **berries** and woodsy **acorns.** Each piece celebrates these gifts from the earth in a time of **harvest** and harboring of **energy.**

Autumn

Morning Brew

MATERIALS

6 medium mums, orange,
  with foliage
4 billy buttons, green
1 small ranunculus, orange
1 small ranunculus, yellow
2 medium ranunculuses,
  orange
2 medium ranunculuses,
  yellow
Styrofoam
Enameled coffeepot with
  spout and handle, red,
  5½" (13.9cm) high with
  a 4"-dia. rim (10.2cm),
  and a 5"-dia. base
  (12.7cm)

TOOLS

Serrated knife
Cutting board
Ruler
Wire cutters

This floral "brew," a profusion of flowers in buttercup yellow and apricot, is accented by flowers in spring green, creating a compact little design that will brighten many days, and inspire smiles. The quirky vintage coffeepot that holds the blooms shows how a little ingenuity can transform a "found" object into a casually-elegant component of a special floral design. Let your imagination run wild when seeking alternatives to traditional vases.

CREATING "MORNING BREW"

1 Place the Styrofoam on the cutting board, and use the serrated knife to trim it to snugly fit inside the coffeepot. Insert the foam into the coffeepot so it rests ½ in.–¾ in. (1.3cm–1.9cm) below the rim.

2 Use wire cutters to cut all stems. Trim the mum stems to 6 in. (15.2cm). Insert the mum stems into the foam around the rim.

3 Cut the billy-button stems to 7 in. (17.8cm). Insert the billy-button stems randomly throughout the arrangement.

4 Trim all ranunculus stems to 7 in. (17.8cm). Use them to fill any remaining spaces in the arrangement. ✐

Tip

Explore flea markets and garage sales to find unusual and exotic containers.

3

4

ESSENTIALS
How to Cut a Wire Stem
    (See page 178.)
How to Make a Multi-Loop
    Bow (See page 186.)

MATERIALS
9 maple leaves, orange
    and yellow, 4" x 5"
    (10.2cm x 12.7cm)
7 oak leaves, green, 2"
    x 5" (5.1cm x 12.7cm)
6 oak leaves, brown, 2"
    x 6" (5.1cm x 15.2cm)
5 oak leaves, orange, 2"
    x 6" (5.1cm x 15.2cm)
1 mulberry-leaf stem,
    brown and green, with
    5 leaves on each of 4
    branches
12 stems of pepperberries,
    deep orange, each with
    about 15 berries
1 stem of winterberries,
    black
7 foam acorns
Floral wire, 24 gauge
Floral tape, green
1½ yds. (1.4m) grosgrain
    ribbon, brown, 1"
    (2.5cm) wide
3 yds. (2.8m) plaid wire-
    edge ribbon, orange-
    and-white, 1½" (3.8cm)
    wide
1½ yds. (1.4m) wire-edge
    ribbon, burgundy, 1½"
    (3.8cm) wide
Twig broom, 22" high x 10"
    wide (55.9cm x 25.4cm)

TOOLS
Ruler
Wire cutters
Scissors
Hot-glue gun and glue
    sticks

Autumn Leaves

A lush gathering of fall leaves

and branches clustered with

berries is the inspired direction of this

fall swag—a colorful profusion of

bronze, orange, and brown foliage that

appears to glow. The branches of crisp leaves, succulent

berries, and plump acorns are bound together, as if for

drying, and then tied together with burgundy and orange-

plaid ribbons. Perfect for displaying on a door, the swag

makes a thoughtful housewarming gift.

 The twig broom is a base for the bundles of leaves and berries. Make the leaf-and-berry bundles wide enough so that large portions of the broom are not exposed. Position the bundles so that they extend beyond the edges of the broom.

CREATING "AUTUMN LEAVES"

1 Before starting, cut five 8-in. (20.3cm) lengths from the winterberry stem. Cut the branches from the mulberry leaf stem. See "Making the Bundles," at right. Make two side bundles, one bottom bundle, one middle bundle, and one top bundle as described. Each bundle should measure 15 in. (38.1cm) long overall, 5 in. (12.7cm) of which is the stem. Use wire cutters to trim off any excess stems. Secure the stems together using floral wire and then floral tape. Set the bundles aside.

2 Position one side bundle on the right side of the broom, as shown. Have the leaves extend beyond the edge of the broom. Secure the bundle to the broom using floral wire. Secure the second side bundle on the left side of the broom.

3 Position the bottom bundle at the center of the bottom of the broom. Allow the leaves to extend beyond the bottom edge of the broom. Secure the bundle to the broom using floral wire.

4 Position the middle bundle in the center of the broom, directly above and overlapping the stem of the bottom bundle. Secure it to the broom using floral wire.

5 Position the top bundle at the base of the broom handle, directly above and overlapping the stem of the middle bundle. Secure it to the broom using floral wire. To wrap the handle, apply a drop of glue to one side of the brown grosgrain ribbon end, and adhere it to the bottom of the broom handle. Working toward the base of the handle, overlap the ribbon while wrapping it tightly. Trim away any excess ribbon, and secure the ribbon end using a drop of glue at the base of the handle.

6 Make a multi-loop bow using the orange-plaid ribbon, and secure it to the base of the handle using wire. Make a smaller multi-loop bow from burgundy ribbon, and use wire to secure it on top of the first bow. Trim the ribbon ends, as desired. ✐

A

B

C

D

Making the Bundles

A. To make a side bundle: Gather one mulberry leaf branch, three brown oak leaves, one green oak leaf, one orange oak leaf, and three pepperberry stems.

B. To make the bottom bundle: Gather three maple leaves, one mulberry-leaf branch, three pepperberry stems, and three winterberry lengths.

C. To make the middle bundle: Gather three maple leaves, one green oak leaf, one orange oak leaf, two acorns, and two winterberry lengths.

D. To make the top bundle: Gather three maple leaves, three pepperberry stems, one mulberry-leaf branch, two orange oak leaves, four green oak leaves, and five acorns.

Tuscan Sunset

MATERIALS

3 stems of maple leaves,
red, orange, and green,
with 3–4 leaves on each
of 3 branches
10 stems of pepperberries,
deep orange, each with
5–7 clusters of berries
3 foam artichokes, green,
with stems, 5" x 5"
(12.7cm x 12.7cm)
6 leucospermums, yellow,
with foliage
3 calla lilies, orange
2 stems of chestnuts with
moss, each with 3
chestnuts
3 stems of acorns and
maple leaves, each with
3 acorns
1 stem of 2 small pears,
with foliage
1 stem of 2 small apples,
with foliage
3 fern fiddleheads, brown
Styrofoam
Bronze urn, with handles,
8½" high (21.6cm) with
a 10"-dia. (25.4cm) rim
and a 4"-square
(10.2cm) base

TOOLS

Serrated knife
Cutting board
Ruler
Wire cutters

The glowing sunsets that one associates with the Tuscan region of Italy inspire the warm fall colors of the floral elements in this majestic design. Built in the style of a sumptuous dome, the Italianate influence of the arrangement is further expressed by the lush accents—fruits, artichokes, and chestnuts—and by the classical bronze loving cup that highlights the flowers. "Tuscan Sunset" evokes the abundance of fall harvest in this southern European area.

CREATING "TUSCAN SUNSET"

1 Place the Styrofoam on the cutting board, and use the serrated knife to trim it to snugly fit inside the urn. Insert the foam into the urn so it rests ½ in.–¾ in. (1.3cm–1.9cm) below the rim.

2 Use wire cutters to cut all stems. Trim the maple leaf branches into 15 5-in. (12.7cm) lengths. Cut the pepperberry stems to 5 in. (12.7cm). Insert the branches and stems around the edge of the urn, as shown, alternating the leaves and berries around the entire rim.

3 Trim the artichoke stems to 5 in. (12.7cm). Insert the stems into the front of the arrangement, spacing them as shown.

4 Cut the leucospermum stems to 7 in. (17.8cm). Insert the leucospermums randomly throughout the arrangement.

(continued on page 102)

5 Trim the calla lily stems to 7 in. (17.8cm). Fill spaces in the arrangement with the calla lilies.

6 Cut the chestnut and the acorn-and-leaf stems to 7 in. (17.8cm). Insert these stems randomly throughout the arrangement to fill the remaining spaces.

7 Trim the pear and apple stems to 6 in. (15.2cm). Insert the pear stem into the back left side. Insert the apple stem into the front left side.

8 Use the wire cutters to trim the fiddlehead stems to 15 in. (38.1cm). Insert the stems into the center of the arrangement. Have the fiddleheads extend above the arrangement so that 2 in.–3 in. (5.1cm–7.6cm) of their stems are visible. ✐

" Flowers have spoken to me more than I can tell in written words. They are the hieroglyphics of angels, loved by all men for the beauty of their character, though few can decipher even fragments of their meaning."
—L. M. Child

7

Tip

Consider adding a small cluster of dried pods or cones to the faux floral elements in "Tuscan Sunset." Use stem wire to secure the cluster, and place it in the arrangement as desired. (See "How to Use Stem Wire and Floral Picks," on page 180.)

8

Kitchen Kitsch

MATERIALS

5 calla lilies, orange
7 small roses, orange
4 small roses, yellow
1 cymbidium orchid stem,
with 2 blooms, yellow
6 stems of pepperberries,
red, with foliage, each
with 5–7 clusters of
berries
2 fern fiddleheads,
green-brown
Styrofoam
Coffee can, 5½" (13.9cm)
high with a 4"
(10.2cm) dia.

TOOLS

Serrated knife
Cutting board
Ruler
Wire cutters

A novel take on recycling, this charming arrangement uses the color of a commercial can that once held aromatic coffee as inspiration. Painted in wide bands of rich orange, yellow, and green, the container cues the selection of lush flowers that cascades over its rim. This brings new meaning to "one man's trash is another man's treasure."

1

2

3

4

5

6

CREATING "KITCHEN KITSCH"

1 Place the Styrofoam on the cutting board, and use the serrated knife to trim it to snugly fit inside the can. Insert the foam into the can so it rests ½ in.–¾ in. (1.3cm–1.9cm) below the rim.

2 Use wire cutters to cut all stems. Trim the calla lily stems to 6 in. (15.2cm). Insert one calla lily stem into the foam in the front center, and another calla lily stem into the back right side. Insert the remaining three stems at graduating heights into the back left side.

3 Cut all rose stems to 7 in. (17.8cm). Separate the roses, varying the colors, into three groups of three and one group of two. Insert the rose clusters throughout the arrangement.

4 Trim the orchid stem to 6 in. (15.2cm). Insert the orchid stem into the front right side.

5 Cut the pepperberry stems to 7 in. (17.8cm). Use them to fill any remaining spaces in the arrangement.

6 Use the wire cutters to trim one fiddlehead stem to 10 in. (25.4cm) and the other to 12 in. (30.5cm). Insert the stems into the center of the arrangement. Have the fiddleheads extend above the arrangement so that 2 in.–3 in. (5.1cm–7.6cm) of their stems are visible. One fiddlehead should be noticeably higher than the other. 🖉

Tip

The perfect container may be as close as your grocery store! Next time you're shopping, notice all of the interesting and colorful packaging.

Welcome Wreath

ESSENTIALS

How to Prepare a
  Container (See page
  176.)
How to Cut a Wire Stem
  (See page 178.)
How to Make a Multi-Loop
  Bow (See page 186.)

MATERIALS

45 foam pears with wire
  stems, green and red,
  1½" x 1½" (3.8cm
  x 3.8cm)
1 winterberry stem, red
4 yds. (3.8m) wire-edge
  organdy ribbon, lime
  green, 2½"-wide
  (6.4cm)
Floral wire, 24 gauge
Floral wire, 20 gauge
Grapevine wreath,
  20"-dia. (50.8cm)

TOOLS

Ruler
Wire cutters
Scissors

Designed to highlight a door or the arch at a front

entrance, this lushly decorated wreath is laden with minia-

ture pears and clusters of red berries that coordinate in

style with the hoops of grapevine that form its foundation.

Providing a graceful counterpoint to the rustic

elegance is a sheer ribbon (in a colorway

that echoes and enhances that of the

pears) that is fastened in a loopy

bow and placed at the top center

of the grapevine wreath.

CREATING THE "WELCOME WREATH"

Note: Use 24-gauge floral wire to secure all stems and bows.

1 Twist the wire stems of five or six pears together to make a cluster. Make six clusters. Begin at the bottom of the grapevine wreath. Secure each cluster to the wreath by twisting the wire stems around one or more strands of vine at the back of the wreath. Further secure the clusters using floral wire if necessary.

2 Fill in any spaces with the remaining pears.

3 Use the wire cutters to cut the winterberry stems into approximately 20 6 in.–8 in. (15.2cm–20.3cm) lengths. Use floral wire to secure the winterberry stems to the grapevine wreath. Position them as shown or as desired.

4 Make a multi-loop bow from the ribbon, and use wire to secure it to the top of the wreath. Trim the ribbon ends as desired. Use 20-gauge floral wire to make a hanging loop, and secure it to the top back of the wreath. ✐

Tip

Faux fruit is a beautiful and long-lasting addition to any wreath. Look for apples, grapes, or pomegranates to enhance your next wreath or door hanging.

~◦≫≪◦~

A ribbon bow can be placed at the top of a wreath as shown in "Welcome Wreath," or it can be placed in any other position, if desired.

"He is happiest who hath power to gather wisdom from a flower."

—*Mary Howitt*

Autumn Sun

MATERIALS

3 cymbidium orchid stems,
   with 3 blooms each,
   green
1 cymbidium orchid stem,
   with 2 blooms each,
   green
3 cymbidium orchid stems,
   with 1 bloom and 2
   buds, green
3 cymbidium orchid stems,
   with 2 blooms each,
   yellow
1 cymbidium orchid stem,
   with 1 bloom and 2
   buds, yellow
Styrofoam
Bronze planter, 6"
   (15.2cm) high with a
   6"-square (15.2cm) rim
   and a 3¼"-square
   (8.3cm) base

TOOLS

Serrated knife
Cutting board
Ruler
Wire cutters

Collecting a single kind of flower and gathering several in a classic mound shape always makes a vivacious style statement. Here, a tight cluster of yellow cymbidium orchids is placed in a bronze-toned container—its softly polished surface highlighting the luminous quality of the crimson-edged petals. Distinctive for their sensual and simple elegance, cymbidium orchids evoke images of the lush tropical environment where they grow naturally.

" Flowers really do intoxicate me."

—— Vita Sackville-West

Tip

Using all of the same type of flower, but in different colors, is an easy way to design an elegant arrangement. Try using other kinds of orchids, roses, lilies, or hydrangeas.

CREATING "AUTUMN SUN"

1 Place the Styrofoam on the cutting board, and use the serrated knife to trim it to snugly fit inside the planter. Insert the foam into the planter so it rests ½ in.–¾ in. (1.3cm–1.9cm) below the rim.

2 Use wire cutters to cut all stems. Trim the orchid stems with three green blooms to 8 in. (20.3cm). Insert the stems into the foam in the center of the arrangement.

3 Cut the remaining green orchid stems to 6 in. (15.2cm). Insert the stems, beginning in the center and working out toward the left side and front left corner.

4 Trim the yellow orchid stems to 6 in. (15.2cm). Insert them into the front right corner and any remaining spaces in the arrangement.

Rustic Chic

ESSENTIALS

How to Prepare a
Container (See page
176.)

How to Cut a Wire Stem
(See page 178.)

MATERIALS

2 stems of hypericum
foliage with berries,
dark green, with 5–6
leaves on each of 2
branches

4 medium ranunculus
stems, yellow

1 calla lily, orange

1 Chinese-lantern stem,
red, orange, and yellow,
with 2 branches

1 poppy, red

1 medium mum, orange

1 mulberry-leaf stem,
brown and green, with
6 leaves on each of 3
branches

2 fern fiddleheads, brown

Floral wire, 24 gauge

Floral tape, medium green

1 piece of coconut bark,
8" x 12" (20.3cm
x 30.5cm)

1½ yds. (1.4m) velvet ribbon, sienna, ⅝" (1.2cm)
wide

TOOLS

Ruler

Wire cutters

Scissors

It's easy to introduce the warm colors of

autumn to your interiors any time of

year. Simply gather flowers, leaves,

and berries in the variegated tones of autumn—rust-

orange, deep eggplant, and warm yellow—and wrap the

floral elements in a bunting of coconut bark. Here, the

simple approach is used to create a bouquet that is both

rustic and chic. Placed on top of a weathered dresser or

on a formal mantle, this romantic fall bouquet reminds us

of home and hearth year-round.

Gathering the Stems

Referring to the photo at left, start in the center, and gather two hypericum-berry branches. Working clockwise from the top, add two ranunculuses, one calla lily, one Chinese-lantern stem, one poppy, the remaining ranunculuses, and one mum. Add the mulberry-leaf branches, spacing them evenly around the bouquet. Then add the remaining hypericum-berry branches and the fiddlehead ferns at the upper left.

CREATING "RUSTIC CHIC"

1 Use wire cutters to cut all stems. Trim all the stems and branches to 12 in. (30.5cm) so they are easier to manage. See "Gathering the Stems" on page 118, and gather the stems into a tight mound.

2 Secure the stems together using floral wire and then floral tape. Trim the stems evenly to 6 in. (15.2cm).

3 Place the coconut bark on the work surface. Position the bouquet in the center of the bark.

4 Wrap the bark around the bouquet, as shown. Secure the coconut bark by wrapping the ribbon around the bark and tying it into a bow.

Tip

Gather the flowers for a bouquet so that the highest point is in the center. The center flowers will have the longest stems. Do not cut the stems too short before they are gathered into a bouquet, so they can be secured together with wire and floral tape. Simply trim them to make them easier to handle.

French Harvest

MATERIALS

2 small sunflowers, with
  foliage, green
4 sunflower-leaf stems (cut
  from sunflower stems),
  each with 2–3 leaves
7 mums, orange, with
  foliage
3 stems of hypericum
  foliage with berries, dark
  red-green, with 5–6
  leaves on each of 2
  branches
3 Chinese-lantern stems,
  red, orange, and yellow,
  with 3–4 lanterns on
  each of 2 branches
Styrofoam
Terra-cotta pot, 7"
  (17.8 cm) high with a
  6¼"-dia. (15.9 cm) rim
  and a 4½"-dia. (11.4 cm)
  base

TOOLS

Serrated knife
Cutting board
Ruler
Wire cutters

The vibrancy of late summer days in the south of France

is the inspiration for this sunny arrangement composed of

a burst of flowers in glowing autumn colors — sunflowers

with earthy-brown centers

surrounded by arrays of

petals in burnt gold, and

Chinese-lantern pods in

bright orange. The terra-

cotta pot completes the

rustic design with panache.

Tip

For an ecclectic mix of textures, distribute the stems of black-eyed susans throughout the arrangement. Their deep-brown centers will add a hint of color.

1

2

3

CREATING "FRENCH HARVEST"

1 Place the Styrofoam on the cutting board, and use the serrated knife to trim it to snugly fit inside the terra-cotta pot. Insert the foam into the pot so it rests ½ in.–¾ in. (1.3cm–1.9cm) below the rim.

2 Use wire cutters to cut all stems. Trim the sunflower stems to 8 in. (20.3cm). Insert one sunflower stem into the foam at the back right side, and the second into the front left side. Bend the stems so the flower heads face out.

3 Cut the mum stems to 8 in. (20.3cm). Insert one mum stem into the center of the foam. Distribute the remaining stems randomly throughout the arrangement.

4 Trim the hypericum-berry branches to 8 in. (20.3cm). Insert the branches around the center mum.

5 Cut the Chinese-lantern branches to 8 in. (20.3cm). Use them to fill any remaining spaces in the arrangement. Position the Chinese-lantern stems slightly higher than the rest of the flowers.

6 Trim the sunflower leaf stems to 8 in. (20.3cm). Insert the stems throughout the arrangement.

Whether
you **dream**
of a **white**
Christmas
spent in a
snowy New
England **town,**
or your idea of
an **evergreen**
is a palm tree
swaying in a
tropical breeze,
we have an
arrangement
to suit your
winter style.

Winter

Christmas Bazaar

MATERIALS

4 large hybrid roses, orange with red accents

4 large roses, yellow

8 medium ranunculuses, yellow

4 small ranunculuses, yellow

2 extra-small ranunculuses, yellow

12 stems of rose leaves, dark green, each with 5 leaves

20 jasmine vines, green

Floral tape

Styrofoam

Beaded bowl, red and gold, 4½" (11.5 cm) high with 7"-dia. (17.7 cm) rim, and 4"-dia. (10cm) base x 4½" (11.5cm) high

TOOLS

Serrated knife

Cutting board

Ruler

Wire cutters

Inspiration often comes from the most unexpected things.

Discovered at a garage sale, this ornate bowl inspired an

arrangement of sumptuous roses and ranunculuses in

yellow and orange, echoing the analogous colorway of

the glittering beads in red and gold. The reflective quality

of the container adds sparkle to holiday

decorating, especially when it is

placed on a dining table and

flanked by shimmering

holiday candles in rich gold.

127

CREATING "CHRISTMAS BAZAAR"

1 Lay the foam on the cutting board, and trim it to fit inside the bowl using a serrated knife. Insert the foam into the bowl so that it fits snugly, ½–¾ in. (1.2cm—1.9cm) below the rim. Use one 8-in. (20.3cm) length of tape to secure the foam to the bowl.

2 Use the wire cutters to trim the stems of the orange roses to 5 in. (12.7cm). Insert one stem into the right center of the foam.

3 Insert another orange rose at the front right side, one at the front left side, and the last at the back left side of the arrangement.

4 Use the wire cutters to trim the length of the stems of the yellow roses to 5 in. (12.7cm). Insert the stems between the orange roses.

5 Use the wire cutters to trim 14 stems of ranunculus to 5 in. (12.7cm). Insert the ranunculus stems into the foam, filling in the spaces between the roses.

6 Use the wire cutters to trim the stems of rose leaves to 5 in. (12.7cm). Insert the stems into the foam, positioning them in any remaining spaces between the roses.

7 Use the wire cutters to trim the stems of jasmine vines to 9 in. (22.7cm). Insert the vines throughout the arrangement, positioning them higher than the rest of the flowers. ✐

1

2

3

4

5

6

" *I perhaps owe having become a painter to flowers.*"

—Claude Monet

7

Silver Snowfall

MATERIALS

4 stems of variegated
myrtle foliage, green-
and-white, with 6–9
leaves on each of
3 branches
2 Casablanca lilies, white,
with foliage
1 large cabbage rose,
white, with foliage
2 lily-bud stems, green,
with foliage, each with
two buds
2 large hydrangeas, white,
with foliage
12 small viburnums, green,
with foliage
8 partially-opened roses,
white, with foliage
Styrofoam
Urn in silver, 6" (15.2cm)
high with an 8"-dia.
(20.3cm) rim

TOOLS

Serrated knife
Cutting board
Ruler
Wire cutters

Ultra-sophisticated, this centerpiece in snowy white and green evokes timeless tradition with its simple but elegant proportions and its subtle contrasts. The shape of the footed bowl in gleaming silver stands as a subtle counterpoint to the textural variety of the flowers and foliage. Arranged primarily in a monochromatic colorway, the arrangement complements both informal and formal decorating schemes.

CREATING "SILVER SNOWFALL"

1 Place the Styrofoam on the cutting board, and use the serrated knife to trim it to snugly fit inside the urn. Insert the foam into the urn so it rests ½ in.–¾ in. (1.3cm–1.9cm) below the rim.

2 Use wire cutters to cut all stems. Trim each variegated-leaf branch to 6 in. (15.2cm). Insert the branches into the foam, creating a loose mound, with the highest point in the center.

3 Cut the lily stems to 8 in. (20.3cm). Insert one lily into the right side of the arrangement and the second into the center.

4 Trim the cabbage rose stem to 8 in. (20.3cm). Insert the stem to the left of the center lily, as shown.

5 Cut the lily-bud stems to 8 in. (20.3cm). Insert one stem into the left side of the arrangement and the second stem into the back.
(continued on page 135)

Tip

White flowers are the perfect choice for a winter wedding or seasonal celebration. Use elegant containers, especially in silver, accenting the arrangement with candles.

4

5

6 Trim the hydrangea stems to 8 in. (20.3cm). Insert one stem into the right side, and the second into the left side.

7 Cut the viburnum stems to 10 in. (25.4cm). Insert them throughout the arrangement. Insert a few at the rim of the urn, and allow them to trail down.

8 Trim the partially-opened rose stems to 8 in. (20.3cm). Insert them, as desired, to fill the remaining spaces, or "holes" in the arrangement.

" The flowers take the tears of weeping night, and give them to the sun for the day's delight."
—Joseph Cotter

Containers and Flowers

It is important to relate the size and shape of a container to the configuration and scale of the flowers and foliage that fills it. In this way, an arrangement with pleasing proportions and balance is created. Here, a low, footed bowl holds a sumptuous mound of floral material echoing the plump curvature of the bowl section of the container. The dome of blooms, upon close inspection, is composed of monochromatic flowers in a wide variety of sizes and shapes—open and just-opened roses, angular lilies, and viburnum florettes—with all elements working together to create a stunning arrangement for any setting.

Hot-Pink Holiday

This unconventional wreath infuses new life into traditional holiday decorating. The secret to its plush texture is the use of hot-pink roses that are crowded together on a foam wreath base. The flower heads conceal the foam and create a lush "carpet" of undulating ruffles of color and texture. For a wall above a fireplace mantle, or an exterior door or entry gate, this wreath is a perfect holiday decoration.

ESSENTIALS
How to Cut a Wire Stem
(See page 178.)

MATERIALS
180 medium garden roses,
hot pink
Floral wire, 20 gauge
Styrofoam wreath base,
white, 18" (45.7cm) in
dia. with a surface area
of 3" (7.6cm)

TOOLS
Wire cutters
Hot-glue gun and glue
sticks

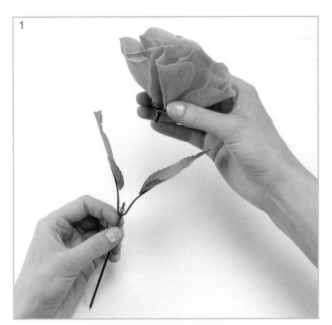

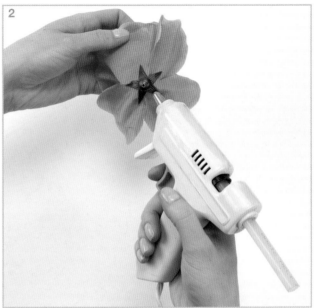

CREATING "HOT-PINK HOLIDAY"

1 Use wire cutters to cut an 18-in. (45.7cm) length of floral wire for the hanger. Wrap the wire once over the edges of the wreath base, ending at the center of one side of the wreath back. Have the wire ends even. Twist the ends together, beginning close to the wreath form. Create a 1-in. loop (2.5cm), ½ in. (1.3cm) from the wreath. To secure the loop, wrap the wire end around the wire under the loop. Trim the end to 2 in. (5.1cm), and insert it into the wreath form at the base of the loop. Remove the roses from their stems. If a flower falls apart, use wire cutters to trim the stem close to the bloom.

2 Apply hot glue to the base of a rose.

3 Before the glue cools, insert the end of the rose base into the foam, on the inside edge of the wreath front. Add roses, butting them to each other on the inside edge until the edge is covered. Use approximately 30 roses.

4 Glue four more rows of roses in the same manner, working toward the outside edge.

" It is at the edge of a petal

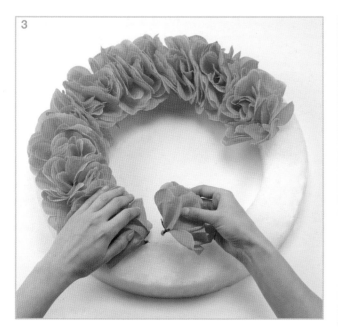

that love waits." — William Carlos Williams

MATERIALS

3 holly-leaf stems, with red berries, with approx. 15 leaves on each of 3 branches

3 variegated holly-leaf stems, with red berries, with approx. 15 leaves on each of 3 branches

6 iced rose-hip stems, with red berries and foliage, each with approx. 15 leaves

6 amaryllis, red, each with 3 blooms

1 stem of pine, with 2 branches and natural pinecones

6 velvet roses, deep burgundy, with foliage

2 large roses, deep burgundy, with leaves, buds, and trailing stems

5 foam pomegranates, red, 3" (7.6cm) in dia.

4 floral picks

Floral tape, medium green

Floral adhesive tape

Styrofoam

Footed bowl in silver, 4" (10.2cm) high with an 11" (27.9cm) dia.

TOOLS

Serrated knife, Cutting board, Ruler, Wire cutters, Scissors, Awl

Happy "Holly" Days

This festive holiday arrangement features classic seasonal flowers arranged in a low spray of rich color. The arrangement is suited to a dining table because it is low enough for guests to see one another from across the table.

The added appeal of the design is the textural variety of smooth pomegranates and holly, rough pinecones, and velvety roses. The arrangement will be an evergreen reminder of many holiday memories.

Tip

If you want to add some color or sparkle to your holiday arrangements, craft stores sell a number of colorful, glossy and glittering floral sprays.

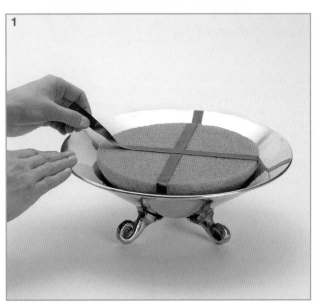

CREATING "HAPPY 'HOLLY' DAYS"

1 Place the Styrofoam on the cutting board, and use the serrated knife to trim it to snugly fit inside the bowl. Insert the foam into the bowl so it rests ½ in.–¾ in. (1.3cm–1.9cm) below the rim. Secure the foam to the bowl with two lengths of floral adhesive tape.

2 Use wire cutters to cut all stems. Trim the holly branches and the rose-hip stems to 9 in. (22.9cm). Insert the branches and stems into the foam, creating a loose mound with the highest point in the center.

3 Cut the amaryllis stems to 8 in. (20.3cm). Insert four stems into the front in an arc, as shown. Insert one stem into the left, and the last stem into the back.

(continued on page 144)

"Flowers always make people better, happier, and more helpful; they are sunshine, food, and medicine to the soul."

—Luther Burbank

4 Trim the evergreen branches to 10 in. (25.4cm). Insert one branch into the right side, and the second into the left side. *Note: Each branch should be positioned immediately above the rim of the bowl.*

5 Cut all rose stems to 8 in. (20.3cm). Insert them randomly into the arrangement.

6 Add floral picks to the pomegranates. Distribute the pomegranates throughout the arrangement. ✐

Tip

Using different kinds of foliage—such as traditional and variegated holly—along with iced rose-hip leaves, creates an arrangement with interesting texture, especially in those where leaves play such a prominent role in establishing the design style.

6

Understated Containers

Although a container plays a central role in the structure of a floral arrangement, it does not have to be glaringly visible to make a design work well. Here, a footed bowl in polished silver provides a low and stable base into which the floral material is arranged. Its polished silver surface reflects light and attractively offsets the rich green foliage and saturated red flowers and berries that rise above it in a lush mound shape. The subtle curve of the bowl bottom is echoed and amplified in the curve of the large-scale flower heads arranged in a broad curve. The combination of gleaming silver and lush color creates an arrangement that is simple and elegant in style.

White Christmas Wreath

Floral elements in icy white configure beautifully in an asymmetrical design, creating an eye-catching seasonal wreath that will welcome guests. The stark contrast between the white colorway of the hydrangea, eucalyptus, and mums, and the natural wood tones of the grapevine wreath highlight the interesting mixture of textures that play against one another in this design. The streamers of a pretty multi-loop bow add a bit of romantic style.

CREATING "WHITE CHRISTMAS WREATH"

Note: Use 24-gauge floral wire to secure all stems and bows.

1 Use wire cutters to cut all stems. Trim the necklace-vine stem to 18 in. (45.7 cm). Position the branches of the vine on the upper right side of the wreath, bending the stem so it follows the curve of the wreath. Secure the stem to the wreath with floral wire.

2 Cut the mum stems to 10 in. (25.4 cm). Separate the mums into two bundles of six. Bind the stems together with floral wire. Secure one mum bundle to the grapevine wreath at the base of the necklace-vine branches. Secure the second bundle below the first.

3 Trim the hydrangeas and hydrangea-leaf stems to 7 in. (17.8 cm). Secure one hydrangea at the base of the second bundle of mums. Secure the leaves below the hydrangea. Position the second hydrangea over the leaves, and secure it with floral wire.

4 Make two multi-loop bows, one from each ribbon. Trim the ribbon ends as desired. Layer the narrower ribbon on the wider ribbon, and secure them to the wreath. Use 20-gauge floral wire to make a hanging loop, and secure it to the top back of the wreath.

Tip

If you can't find iced flowers, make your own! Simply brush white craft glue onto faux flowers, and sprinkle them with fake snow, which can be found in most craft stores. For more sparkle, add a dusting of silver glitter, too!

Southern Hospitality

MATERIALS

3 stems of spruce, green,
  each with 3 branches
  and cones
3 stems of pine, green,
  each with side branches
  and pinecones
3 cymbidium-orchid
  stems, red, each with
  two blooms and two
  buds
8 medium roses, red,
  with foliage
3 holly-leaf stems, green
  with red berries, with
  approx. 15 leaves on
  each of 3 branches
Styrofoam
Mint-julep cup, silver, 7½"
  (19.1cm) high with a
  4½" (11.4cm) dia.

TOOLS

Serrated knife
Cutting board
Ruler
Wire cutters

Inspired by gracious southern tradition, this arrangement

begins with a mint-julep cup in polished silver. The cup

adds a festive glow and highlights the generous gathering

of rich red flowers and green foliage of the season that

rises above its rim—velvety roses, lustrous cymbidium

orchids, evergreen branches topped

with cones, and holly berries. Easy

to arrange, "Southern Hospitality" will

add a warm note of seasonal welcome

when placed in an entry foyer.

CREATING "SOUTHERN HOSPITALITY"

1 Place the Styrofoam on the cutting board, and use the serrated knife to trim it to snugly fit inside the mint-julep cup. Insert the foam into the cup so it rests ½ in.–¾ in. (1.3cm–1.9cm) below the rim.

2 Use wire cutters to trim the spruce branches to 13 in. (33cm). Insert them into the foam, creating a loose mound, with the highest point in the center.

3 Cut the pine branches to 15 in. (38.1cm). Insert one branch into the center of the arrangement. Insert one branch

to the right of the center branch and one to the left, creating a fan shape. Insert the last branch into the back center.

4 Trim the orchid stems to 8 in. (20.3cm). Insert the stems into the center front of the arrangement.

5 Cut the rose stems to 10 in. (25.4cm). Position a cluster of roses at the front, as shown. Then insert the rest of the stems throughout the arrangement.

6 Trim the holly branches to 10 in. (25.4cm). Insert the branches randomly into the arrangement. ✍

Tip

Red and green are the traditional holiday colors, but instead of poinsettias, be imaginative. Combine any red flower with ever-green to create a new and innova-tive arrangement for your holiday celebration.

MATERIALS

2 stems of mint leaves, light green, with approx. 15 leaves on each of 4 branches

3 stems of rosemary, dark green, each with 5 branches

1 bunch of cilantro, light green

3 small velvet roses, deep burgundy

3 stems of pokeberries, burgundy with foliage, each with 3 branches

2 stems of oregano with foliage, each with 3 branches

2 branches of chestnuts with moss, each with 1 chestnut

4 floral picks

Floral tape, medium green

1 yd. (0.9m) of raffia

2 pieces of coconut bark, 8" x 12" (20.3cm x 30.5cm)

Double-sided tape, 1" wide (2.5cm)

Styrofoam

Heavy glass container, 5" (12.7cm) high and 5" (12.7cm) square

TOOLS

Serrated knife, Cutting board, Ruler, Wire cutters, Scissors

Winter Herb Garden

Lush garden herbs accented by berry stems form a crown around the heads of full-blown roses in dramatic burgundy. Billowing out in a loosely arranged design, the floral elements are "planted" in a container that is concealed in rough-textured coconut bark. What is outstanding about the design is that common herbs appear so elegant when paired with roses. A perfect accent for a kitchen or sunroom, this herb garden will "bloom" all year long.

CREATING "WINTER HERB GARDEN"

1 Cover the container with coconut bark tied with raffia. Place the Styrofoam on the cutting board, and use the serrated knife to trim it to snugly fit inside the container. Insert the foam into the container so it rests ½ in.–¾ in. (1.3cm–1.9cm) below the rim.

2 Use wire cutters to cut all stems. Trim the mint-leaf branches to 9 in. (22.9cm). Insert the branches into the foam, creating a loose mound, with the highest point in the center.

3 Cut the rosemary branches to 9 in. (22.9cm). Distribute the branches throughout the center of the arrangement.

4 Trim the cilantro stems to 6 in. (15.2cm). Bundle the stems into a fan shape, and use floral tape to bind them together onto a floral pick. Trim the overall length to 9 in. (22.9cm). Insert the cilantro into the center of the arrangement.
(continued on page 158)

" Almost any garden, if you see it at
just the right moment,
can be confused with paradise."
—Henry Mitchell

Basic geometric shapes can guide the placement of flowers and keep an arrangement balanced and interesting. Here, herb clusters frame the burgundy roses, which are placed in a triangular configuration.

5 Cut the rose stems to 7 in. (17.8cm). Insert the stems into the front, in a triangle shape, as shown.

6 Separate the pokeberry branches into three bundles, and use floral tape to bind them together onto floral picks. Trim the overall length to 10 in. (25.4cm). Insert one bundle into the center, behind the roses. Insert the remaining pokeberries on both sides of the roses.

7 Trim the oregano branches to 9 in. (22.9cm). Insert them around the roses or as desired.

8 Cut the chestnut branches to 9 in. (22.9cm). Insert one branch into the right side and the other into the left side. 🌿

Making Majestic Multiples

Small-scale arrangements can be transformed into ones that have larger proportions and more stylistic presence by making more than one of them and arranging them in a group. Applying this principle is most successful when working with rectilinear containers that can be pushed together to create the impression that the multiple arrangements are one design. The design principle can be applied to round containers, but the configuration reveals the construction "secret." To make a more bountiful "Winter Herb Garden" display, apply the construction principles explained in the featured design to create as many as needed to decorate the length of the display space (such as a long table or fireplace mantle). Line up the arrangements for a rich textural display during the winter months.

7

Tip

Substitute ranunculuses for the roses in this arrangement for a spring-time design that has bright color. Change the roses to mums in autumn.

8

the
Essentials
of Floral Design

Although imagination is, first and foremost, the most

essential requirement of effective floral design, there are

important fundamentals that are necessary if an arrange-

ment is to be pleasing to the eye and structurally sound.

In this section, those basics are elaborated upon in easy-

to-follow directions and photographs. Refer to "The

Essentials" often to familiarize yourself with the tools,

materials, and techniques that inform the designing

process. This foundation will give you the knowledge and

confidence to create stunning floral arrangements of your

own design.

TOOLS

1 Ruler
2 Cutting board
3 Awl
4 Serrated knife
5 Scissors
6 Wire cutters

MATERIALS

1 Styrofoam
2 Floral foam
3 White glue
4 Glass cleaner
5 Rocks
6 Stem wire
7 Floral picks
8 Floral wire
9 Floral pins
10 Toothpicks
11 Floral clay
12 Hot-glue gun and
glue sticks
13 Soap
14 Floral "frogs"
15 Floral adhesive tape
16 Floral stem-wrap tape
17 Double-stick tape

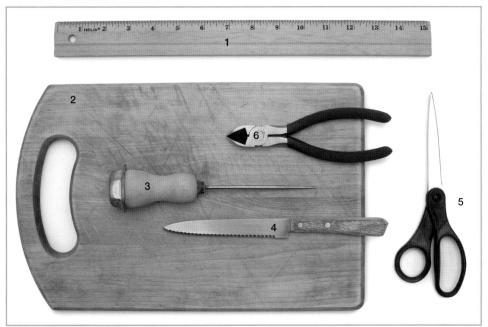

Tools
and
Materials

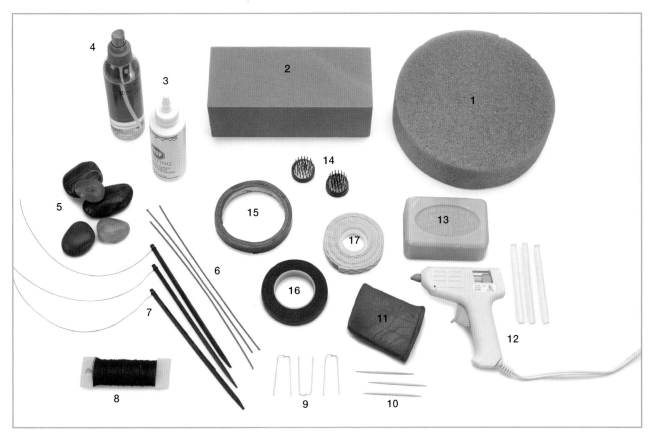

An Illustrated Glossary of Spring Flowers and Foliage

Leucospermum

Cymbidium orchids

Rose

Lemons

Hypericum foliage

Lemon foliage

Ranunculuses

Ranunculuses

Peony

Rose

Stargazer lily

Rose

Rose foliage

Ranunculus

Jasmine vine

Lily bud

"*More than anything, I must have flowers… always, always…*"

—*Claude Monet*

Hydrangea

Galax leaf

Nigella

Dutch iris

Casablanca lilies

Hydrangea

Hydrangea

Pompon mums

Anemone

Viburnum

Rose

Parrot tulip

Banana leaf

Allium

Viburnum

Ranunculuses

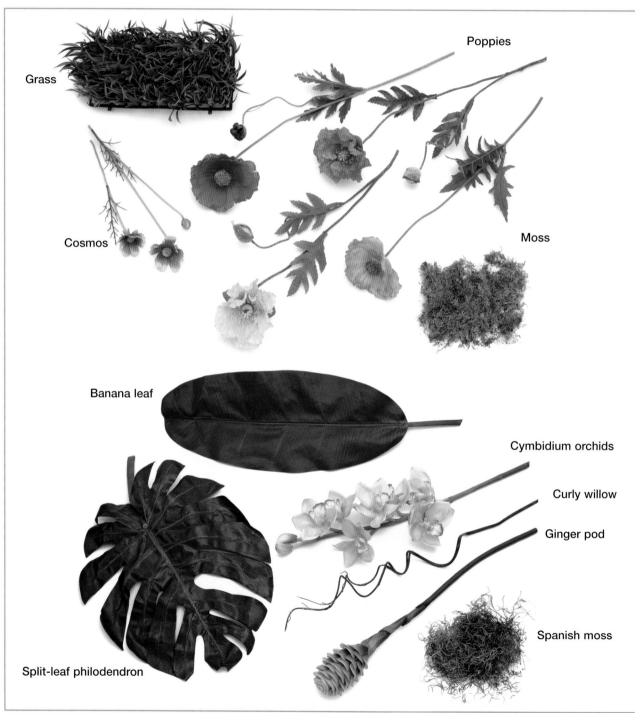

Grass

Poppies

Cosmos

Moss

Banana leaf

Cymbidium orchids

Curly willow

Ginger pod

Spanish moss

Split-leaf philodendron

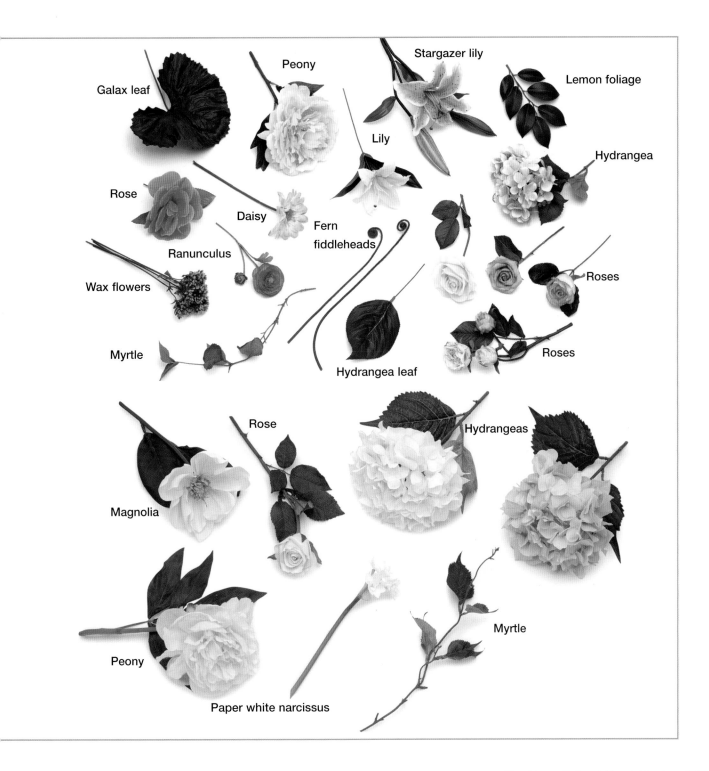

Galax leaf

Peony

Stargazer lily

Lemon foliage

Lily

Hydrangea

Rose

Daisy

Fern fiddleheads

Roses

Ranunculus

Wax flowers

Roses

Myrtle

Hydrangea leaf

Roses

Rose

Hydrangeas

Magnolia

Peony

Myrtle

Paper white narcissus

Chestnuts

Hypericum

Oregano

Pears

Pepperberry

Acorns

Pepperberry

Artichoke

Fern fiddleheads

Pepperberry

Winterberry

Apple

Pears

Pepperberry

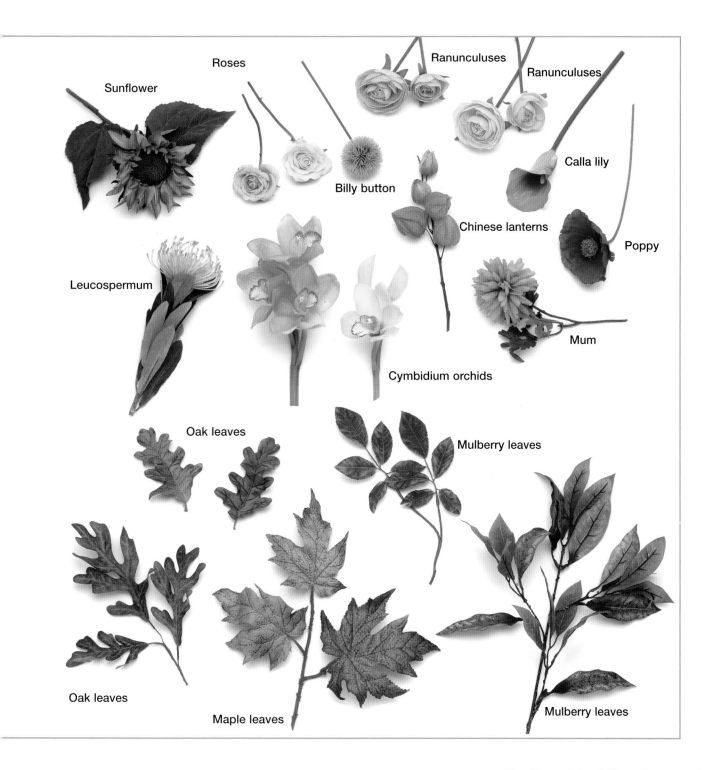

Roses

Ranunculuses

Ranunculuses

Sunflower

Billy button

Calla lily

Chinese lanterns

Poppy

Leucospermum

Mum

Cymbidium orchids

Oak leaves

Mulberry leaves

Oak leaves

Maple leaves

Mulberry leaves

Amaryllis

Rose

Cymbidium orchids

Pokeberries

Iced holly

Spruce

Pine

Rose

Oregano

Pomegranates

Chestnut

Iced rose hips

Holly

Iced hydrangea

Hydrangea

Iced necklace vine

Casablanca lily

Mums

Rose

Rose

Viburnum

Mint leaves

Rosemary

Cilantro

Rose

Variegated leaves

Rose

Rose

Rose

Rose

Ranunculuses

Rose foliage

Rose foliage

An Illustrated Glossary of Containers by Season

Spring

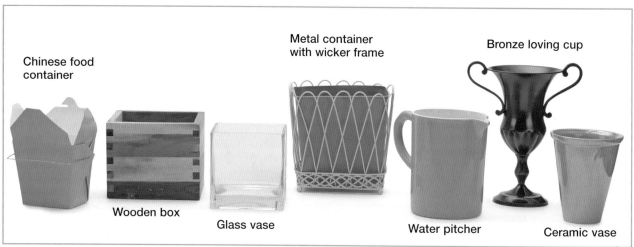

Chinese food container

Wooden box

Glass vase

Metal container with wicker frame

Water pitcher

Bronze loving cup

Ceramic vase

Summer

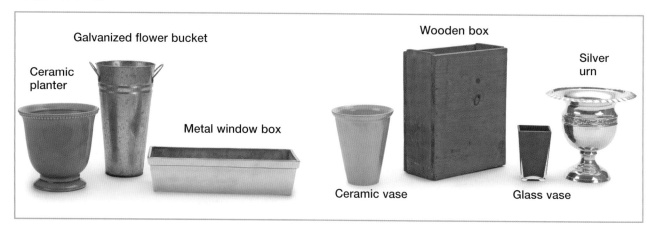

Ceramic planter

Galvanized flower bucket

Metal window box

Ceramic vase

Wooden box

Glass vase

Silver urn

Autumn

Enameled coffee-pot

Coffee can

Bronze urn

Bronze planter

Twig broom

Coconut bark

Terra-cotta pot

Grapevine wreath

Winter/Holiday

Beaded bowl

Footed bowl

Silver urn

Styrofoam wreath

Grapevine wreath

Silver urn

Glass vase

Mint-julep cup

Techniques

The techniques described here are used throughout the book. But here, they are presented in greater detail. Refer to the directions and detailed photographs to ensure good results when creating your faux floral arrangements.

How to Cut Foam

HOW TO CUT STYROFOAM

1 For ease of cutting, run a bar of soap along both sides of the blade of the serrated knife.

2 Position the container on the Styrofoam, base side down. Use a marker to trace around the container's perimeter.

3 Use the serrated knife to cut along the marked line, angling the blade outward if the container's rim is wider than the base.

4 Test-fit the foam inside the container, trimming away any excess foam, if necessary.

Tip

Cutting Styrofoam is not an exact procedure. It is advisable to test-fit the foam inside the container to ensure a snug fit. If the foam is too large, slice away small amounts using a serrated knife until the foam fits snugly. If the foam is cut too small, simply wedge as many small pieces of foam between the wall of the container and the foam block as needed to create a snug fit.

HOW TO CUT A CIRCULAR DISK OF STYROFOAM

If you will need a circular disk of Styrofoam, you can:

A Purchase a manufactured piece in a circular shape from your local craft store. If it is a perfect fit, use it as is. If not, use a serrated knife to shave off the excess foam, test-fitting the piece in your container until it fits snugly inside.

B Follow the directions on page 172 for "How To Cut Styrofoam," resting the container on the foam, rim side down, tracing around the container, and cutting along the marked line with a serrated knife.

   1 Begin with a square piece of Styrofoam that is large enough to fit within the container. Trim the corners with a serrated knife until the piece fits within the container.

   2 Round the edges using the serrated knife. Frequently test-fit the Styrofoam until it fits inside the container.

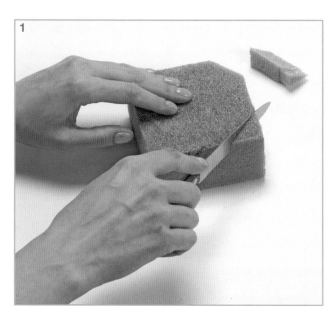

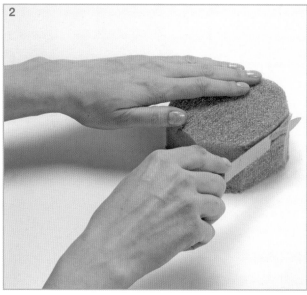

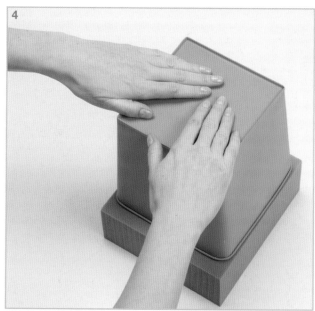

HOW TO CUT FLORAL FOAM

Floral foam, also called Oasis, comes in smaller brick-shaped blocks, so it is often necessary to use more than one block to accommodate containers with large openings. Assess how many blocks of floral foam are necessary to create a surface area that is large enough for the opening of the container. If it is more than one, follow steps 1–3. Then follow steps 4–6 to cut the floral foam.

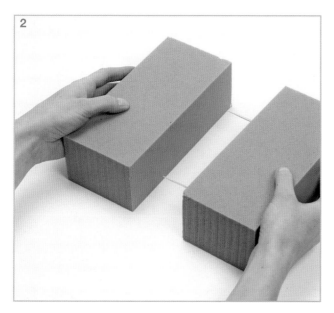

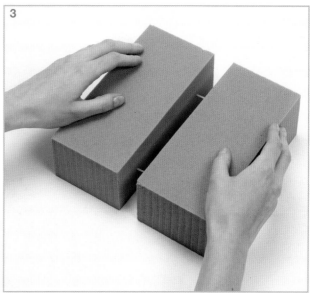

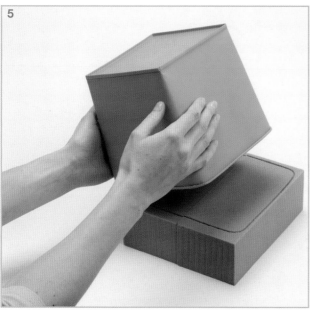

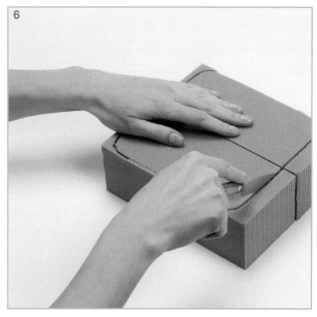

1 To join two blocks of floral foam together, insert tooth-picks into the side of one block.

2 Place a second block next to the first with the toothpicks in between, lining up the top and bottom edges of the blocks.

3 Join the blocks by pushing them together until their sides are flush against one another.

4 Position the opening of the container on the floral foam.

5 Push down on the container to create an impression in the foam. Lift the container off the foam, and set it aside.

6 Using the impression in the foam as a guideline, cut away the excess foam using the serrated knife. Test-fit the foam inside the container, shaving off any excess until the foam fits snugly.

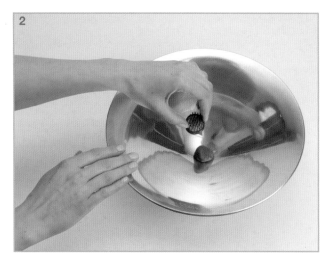

How to Prepare the Container

HOW TO SECURE FOAM IN A CONTAINER

When working with shallow containers, especially those made of metal, it is necessary to establish an anchor for the foam if it is to remain stable and support the floral materials. Measure and cut the foam; then follow these steps before inserting it into the container.

1 Tear off a wad of floral clay about 1 in. (2.5cm) in diameter. Place the wad in the bottom of the container, and press it down until it adheres.

2 Position and press the floral "frog" into the clay to secure it.

3 Place the pre-cut piece of foam into the container, and push it down until the prongs on the frog pierce the foam.

4 Measure and cut two lengths of floral adhesive tape equal in length to the measurement of the span across the top of the container plus 2 in. (5cm). Stretch the lengths of tape across the container at a perpendicular angle, and secure the ends to the sides.

HOW TO STABILIZE A TALL CONTAINER

Taller containers can be unstable, especially if heavy floral material extends above their rims. To lower the center of gravity, it may be necessary to add weight to the base of the container to keep it from falling over when the floral material is inserted.

Place a few handfuls of rocks or pebbles in the bottom of the container. Then proceed to fill it with foam if the arrangement requires it.

" Flowers are like human beings...they thrive on a little kindness"

— Fred Streeter

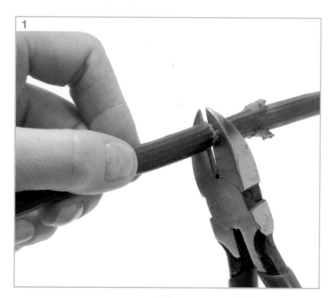

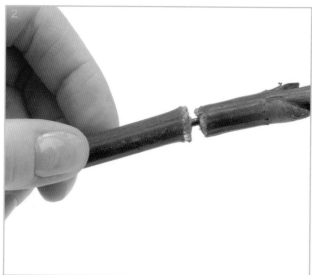

How to Cut a Wire Stem

TO SHORTEN THE MAIN STEM

The following steps provide helpful methods for cutting thick stems that have strong interior wires.

1 Use the wire cutters to grasp the stem. Rotate the stem while gripping it with the jaws of the cutters to cut through the plastic coating on the main stem.

2 Continue cutting away the plastic coating on the stem to reveal the wire.

3 Score the circumference of the wire using the jaws of the wire cutters.

4 Hold the stem sections and rock them back and forth until the wire snaps in half.

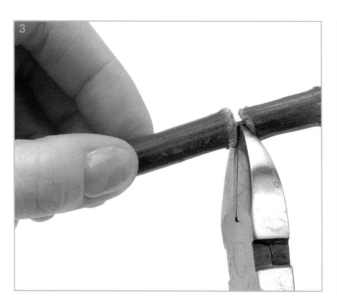

TO CUT A BLOOM OR LEAF FROM A STEM

1 Use the wire cutters to remove the bloom from the stem, cutting the main stem close to the leaves. Set the bloom aside. Note: To cut off a single leaf, cut the leaf stem close to the main stem.

2 Trim the wire near the leaves to a nub, if further trimming is necessary, and insert the leafy stem into the arrangement.

How to Use Stem Wire and Floral Picks

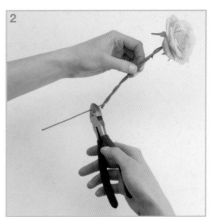

TO STRENGTHEN A STEM

Certain stems cannot be directly inserted into Styrofoam because they are too fragile or flexible to pierce the foam. Stem wire can also help to strengthen them.

1 Lay a stem wire against the stem of the flower. Hold the stem wire against the flower stem just beneath the head of the flower, and begin to wind the wire around the stem.

2 Continue to wind the wire around the entire length of the stem. Use the wire cutters to cut any excess wire.

Styrofoam is noted for its stiffness, and it is suited to large arrangements of floral materials that have weight and height. For a small arrangement of lightweight floral-materials, even those with fragile stems, substitute floral foam for the Styrofoam. It is much easier to work with.

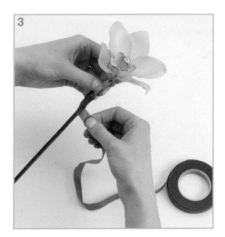

TO LENGTHEN A STEM

Flowers or leaves with short stems can be used in arrangements that call for floral material with longer stems by simply lengthening their stems using floral picks.

1 Lay the floral pick on the flower stem so they overlap.

2 Wind the wire on the floral pick around the stem and the pick to secure them together.

3 Conceal the stem and the pick by wrapping them with floral stem-wrap tape.

TO MAKE A FLORAL CLUSTER

To create a cluster of small or delicate elements for use in an arrangement, secure single stems in a group instead of inserting them into the arrangement one element at a time.

1   Gather the stems of foliage or flowers together, arranging their heads in a fan shape if desired.

2   Lay the floral pick against the bottom third of the stems, and wrap the wire firmly around the pick and the stems.

3   Wrap the stems and the pick using floral stem-wrap tape.

" All seasons are beautiful to the person who carries happiness within" — Horace Freiss

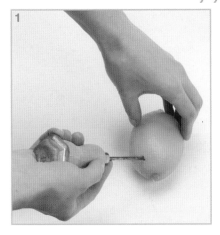
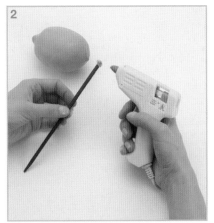

TO ADD A "STEM" TO A PIECE OF FRUIT

Foam fruit and vegetables can be unique additions to any arrangement. Some have wire stems, but many do not. To add a stem to a piece of fruit or a vegetable, use a floral pick.

1   Carefully use an awl to pierce a small hole in the side of the foam fruit.

2   Remove the wire from the floral pick. Apply a small drop of hot glue to the end of the floral pick.

3   Insert the glued end of the floral pick into the hole in the fruit. Let the glue cool.

How to Wrap Foam with Foliage

To create the elegant wrapped-leaf look seen in "Simply Modern," on page 29, follow these steps:

1 Measure and cut a piece of foam to fit within the container.

2 Place the foam on its side on a flat work surface. Secure one end of the banana leaf to the foam using a floral pin.

3 Wrap the leaf around the block of foam, keeping it flush against the surface. Overlap the ends, securing them with a floral pin.

4 Carefully slide the wrapped block of foam into the vase.

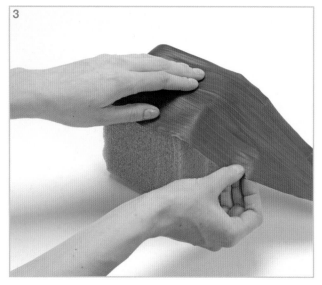

How to Wrap a Container with Coconut Bark

To create the same beautiful vase featured in "Winter Herb Garden," on page 154, follow these steps:

1 Apply a strip of double-stick tape around the bottom of the vase ½ in. (1.2cm) above the edge. Repeat to apply tape around the vase top 1 in. (2.5cm) below the rim.

2 Peel off the protective paper from the tape. Center the vase on the coconut bark. Wrap one side of the bark up and over the vase, and bring it to the center. Press down to adhere the bark to the vase. Repeat on the opposite side.

3 Use scissors to trim the ends of the bark flush with the top and bottom edges of the vase.

4 Cut two ¾-yd. (68.6cm) lengths of raffia. Center one strand on the vase 1 in. (2.5cm) above the bottom edge. Bring the ends around to the back and to the front again, tying the ends in a double knot. Center the second strand 1 in. (2.5cm) below the rim.

5 Bring the ends to the back and to the front again, tying them in a double knot.

6 Trim the raffia ends.

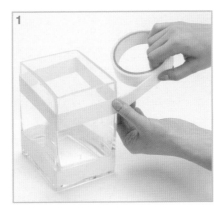

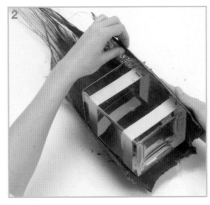

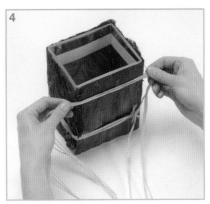

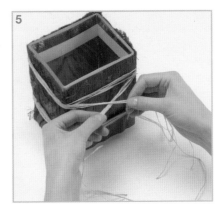

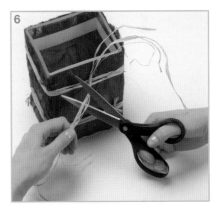

Tip

If one leaf isn't long or wide enough, overlap a second (or third) leaf on the previously laid leaves to ensure that the foam is concealed.

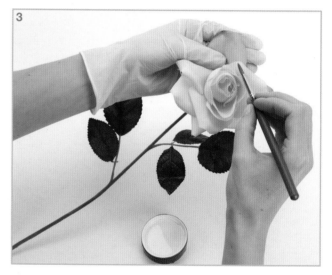

How to Create a New Variety

USING COLORED MARKERS

Washable colored markers can be used to revitalize the color of faded faux flowers or to create a completely new variety. To create a variegated rose, follow these steps:

1 Put on one rubber glove. Hold the end of one fabric petal in your gloved hand, and use a paintbrush dipped in plain water to saturate the fabric.

2 Using a colored marker in a shade slightly darker than the color of the petals, draw on the outside edge of the petal.

3 Dip the paintbrush in water, and use it to blend the color on the petal. Then continue to blend it in by rubbing the petal between your gloved fingers.

4 Repeat steps 1–3 to add color to the tips of the remaining petals. For added detail, use the marker to draw on the edges of the petals at the center bud.

USING PAINT

Paint can be used to add rich details to faux flowers. To transform a plain tulip into a parrot tulip, follow these steps:

1 Put on one rubber glove. In a small lid, mix a few drops of water and red-orange watercolor paint using a brush. Run the bristles on a paper towel so they are not dripping. Hold one petal in your gloved hand. Beginning at the center of the petal's base, paint a short line. Add feathery strokes that extend from the line to the sides of the petal.

2 Continue to add feathery strokes using the brush and red-orange paint, thickening the central decoration as shown.

3 Fill in an irregular band of the color at the tip of the petal, adding saturated color to the edge.

4 Repeat steps 1–3 to paint the remaining petals. Let the paint dry.

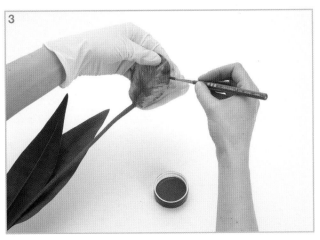

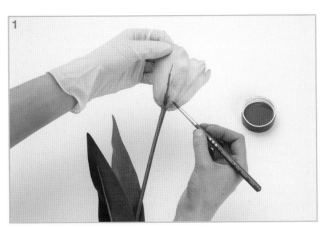

How to Make a Multi-Loop Bow

A mult-loop bow looks great on floral arrangements, especially on wreaths. Making one is easy, but it does require a bit of practice. For foolproof results, choose wire-edged ribbon; it holds its shape and comes in a wide array of colors, patterns, and widths. The key to making a neat, well-proportioned bow is making the loops equal in size. Once you have mastered the technique, you can make a multi-loop bow with up to 20 loops.

1   Measure and cut a 2-yd. length (1.8m) of ribbon. Tie the ribbon around the base of the wreath, and make a single knot. Leave only enough ribbon on the right streamer to make one loop and a tail. Leave the remaining yardage on the left.

2   Release the loop on the right and move it to the side. It will not be used again until step 6. On the left side, make one loop with the ribbon by moving the ribbon away from you and then back over itself until it reaches the center knot. Grip the loop at the knot with your thumb and two fingers.

3   While continuing to hold the original loop with your left hand, use your right hand to extend the ribbon toward your body and back over itself until it reaches the center knot, creating a loop. This loop should be equal in length and a mirror image of the first. Grip this loop over the knot, and hold it with the original loop using your left hand.

4   Repeat step 2 to create another loop.

5   Repeat step 3 to create another loop. Continue by repeating steps 4–5

until there are seven loops on the top and six loops on the bottom.

6   Without letting go of the loops in your left hand, use your right hand to pick up the short ribbon on the right side.

Tip

After you have tied your multi-loop bow, open up each loop so it is a neat oval. Arrange the loops in a voluminous arc or a ball shape according to the style of your floral arrangement and the desired location of the bow.

7 Bring the short ribbon over the center knot. Do not let go of the looped ribbons in the left hand.

8 Still using the right hand, bring the short ribbon under the left hand. Drop the short ribbon from the right hand; reach around from the opposite side; and pull the ribbon toward the inside of the wreath.

9 Make a loop at the midpoint with the short ribbon using the right hand. Pull the loop through the ribbon hole made in steps 7–8.

10 Pull the loops in your left hand and the loop in your right hand at the same time to tighten the knot in the middle. If the right loop is too large, adjust it by pulling the end of the short ribbon only.

11 To change the orientation of the bow, twist it at the knot. The long ribbon that was on the left will now be on the right.

12 Bring the short ribbon under the loops on the left side of the bow and opposite the long ribbon. Cut the ends.

*"The old tree is shook,
white blossoms slowly float down,
dancers in the wind"*
— Alexandra Kim

How to Care for Silk Flowers

Here are a few rules of thumb to keep your faux floral arrangements looking fresh and new for a long time.

✐ Display your arrangements in areas that are cool and dry.

✐ Avoid exposing floral materials to direct sunlight, heat from baseboard radiators or heat registers, and high humidity.

✐ When not displayed, keep your floral arrangements stored in a dimly lit, dry space, covering them loosely to keep them from accumulating dust.

HOW TO FIX FRAYED EDGES

When silk flowers begin to fray, use these simple steps to preserve them.

1 Use sharp scissors to carefully trim away any stray threads.

2 Apply a scant dab of glue along the trimmed edge, and use your finger to spread the glue into the woven fabric. Let the glue dry.

HOW TO REMOVE DUST

✐ Use a hair dryer set to "cold" and "low" to blow air through the petals until there is no visible dust. Work in a well-ventillated space, preferably out-doors.

✐ Large leaves with a fine plastic coating may be wiped with a damp cloth.

✐ If the label on the stem of the flower or foliage indicates that the fabric is synthetic, dip it into warm water, and allow the bloom to dry completely.

Tip

Dabbing glue to the edges of silk flowers can also be used preventively.

Sources and Resources

AFLORAL.COM
165 Jones and Gifford Ave.
Jamestown, NY 14701
888-299-4100
www.alfloral.com

SAVE-ON-CRAFTS
831-768-8428
www.save-on-crafts.com

JAMALI GARDEN HARDWARE
149 W. 28th St.
New York, NY 10001
212-244-4025
www.jamaligarden.com

PANY SILK FLOWERS
146 W. 28th St.
New York, NY 10001
212-645-9526

USI FLORAL INC.
2910 S. Alameda St.
Vernon, CA 90058
877-874-1818
www.usifloral.com

**OXFORD GROVE
PREMIUM ARTIFICIAL PLANTS**
P.O. Box 308
1877 Mallard Lane
Klamath Falls, OR 97601
503-922-0511
www.oxfordgrove.com

FLOWERS BY DESIGN
470 Mission St., Unit #11
Carol Stream, IL 60188
630-665-9333
1-800-833-SILK
www.flowers-by-design.com

MICHAELS, THE ARTS AND CRAFTS STORE
8000 Bent Branch Dr.
Irving, TX 75063
800-642-4235
www.michaels.com

E-SILK FLOWER DEPOT
5110 W. Knox St.
Tampa, FL 33634
800-444-2920
www.e-silkflowerdepot.com

Index

If you like **Faux Florals,**
take a look at other titles in our Home Arts Line

Bead Style is a fun and funky collection of fabulous jewelry made in the chunky style using beads of every description.
- 50 gorgeous pieces including bracelets, necklaces, and rings
- Over 150 full-color photographs
- The essential "Beading Basics" so that anyone can make every piece in "The Collection"
- An easel-back, spiral-bound book that allows "hands free" access to all of the information

Bead Style
ISBN: 1-58011-314-4
UPC: 0-78585-11314-9
CH Book # 265147
128 pages, 8" x 10⅞"
$19.95 US / $24.95 CAN

Quilt Style
ISBN: 1-58011-332-X
UPC: 0-78585-11332-3
CH Book # 265193
128 pages, 8" x 10⅞"
$19.95 US / $24.95 CAN

Quilt Style is a stunning collection of quilts made in today's fresh colors and contemporary style.
- 18 gorgeous projects with an additional 18 variations that suit every decorating style
- For beginner and veteran quilters alike
- Over 400 color photographs and diagrams
- A comprehensive mini-course in quilting, "Quilting Basics," and "Sources and Resources"
- An easel-back, spiral-bound book that allows "hands free" access to all of the information

The Decorated Bag is a fun and stylish collection of 50 bags that are decorated using embellishments such as sparkling rhinestones, jewelry, and ribbons and trims of every kind.
- Over 175 original full-color photographs accompanied by directions for all of the decorative techniques, suited to all skill levels, especially the beginner
- 25 beautiful and stylish bags PLUS another 25 design variations, including patterns for making the clutch, pull-string, and tote-style designs from scratch
- Author, Genevieve A. Sterbenz, is a nationally-known designer and television personality.

The Decorated Bag
ISBN: 1-58011-296-X
UPC: 0-78585-11296-8
CH Book # 265138
144 pages, 8½" x 9½"
$19.95 US / $24.95 CAN

Glamorous Beaded Jewelry
ISBN: 1-58011-295-1
UPC: 0-78585-11295-1
CH Book # 265133
144 pages, 8½" x 9½"
$19.95 US / $24.95 CAN

Glamorous Beaded Jewelry presents a stunning collection of 25 fun and sophisticated beaded originals—from bracelets and necklaces to rings and earrings that suit every style and occasion.
- Over 175 original color photographs of the stunning designs, and easy-to-follow step-by-step directions
- Features chunky bracelets, knotted and bejewelled chokers, chandelier earrings, lariat-style necklaces, crystal rings, and much, much more
- Special sections, including "Beading Basics" and "Sources and Resources," that guarantee near professional-looking results in jewelry-making